HOME OFFICE RESEARCH STUDY NO. 111

The 1988 British Crime Survey

by Pat Mayhew, David Elliott and Lizanne Dowds

A HOME OFFICE
RESEARCH AND PLANNING UNIT
REPORT

LONDON: HER MAJESTY'S STATIONERY OFFICE

First published 1989

ISBN 0 11 340965 6

HOME OFFICE RESEARCH STUDIES

"Home Office Research Studies" comprise reports on research undertaken in the Home Office to assist in the exercise of its administrative functions, and for the information of the judicature, the services for which the Home Secretary has responsibility (direct or indirect), and the general public.

On the last pages of this report are listed titles already published in this series, in the preceding series Studies in the Causes of Delinquency and the Treatment of Offenders, and in the series of Research and Planning Unit Papers.

Foreword

This report presents some of the main findings from the third British Crime Survey (BCS), which was carried out early in 1988. Two earlier sweeps were carried out in 1982 and 1984. The BCS offers information about the nature and extent of selected crimes, and the different groups at risk. It covers crime both recorded and unrecorded by the police, providing an additional measure of crime to be set alongside offences recorded by the police.

This third BCS shows that, overall, crime as measured by the BCS has risen significantly less since 1981 (by 30%) than offences recorded by the police (41%). This shows that some of the increase in recorded crime since 1981 has been due to more of the offences which people experience finding their way into police records both because victims are generally reporting more offences, and the police may be recording more.

Besides estimating the level of crime, each sweep of the BCS has covered a number of additional crime-related topics. This report is not a full description of the survey's findings, but some of the main topics in the 1988 survey which are covered are: victimisation at work, participation in Neighbourhood Watch schemes, and risks of crime among ethnic minorities (made possible by special sampling). As was done with previous surveys, several detailed reports will be prepared on other topics covered in the 1988 sweep.

MARY TUCK
Head of the Research and Planning Unit

July 1989

Acknowledgements

The third British Crime Survey involved much effort by many people. Thanks are due first to those in NOP Market Research and Social and Community Planning Research who were involved in the survey's development and execution. At NOP, Nick Moon and Richard Glendenning made an invaluable input, as did Douglas Wood and Nigel Tremlett at SCPR. Douglas Wood, who was overall co-ordinator of the survey, died on the last day of 1988. His work on the BCS (he also took part in the 1982 survey) was testimony to his great survey skills. Colin Airey at SCPR was very helpful after Douglas's death in dealing with SCPR's responsibilities for the survey.

Thanks are also due to a number of academics who were invited to advise on the coverage of the 1988 BCS, and on how best to deal with particular topics:
Trevor Bennett, Steven Box, Norman Davidson, Chris Hale, Brian Hilton, Sohail Husain, Richard Kinsey, Mike Maguire, Rob Mawby, Jane Morgan, Rod Morgan, Ken Pease, John Pointing, Joanna Shapland, David Smith, Susan Smith, Betsy Stanko, Mollie Weatheritt, and Paul Wiles.

Within the Home Office, many colleagues also played a part in the design of the survey and in advising on this report. In particular, Mike Hough, who was very closely involved in the two previous sweeps, made a substantial contribution and was very largely responsible for the design of the component on contacts with the police. We are also grateful to Roger Tarling and Mary Tuck for their patience while this report was being prepared.

LIZANNE DOWDS
DAVID ELLIOTT
PAT MAYHEW

Contents

1 Introduction

This report presents results from the third sweep of the British Crime Survey for England and Wales (BCS), which was conducted early in 1988. The survey questions a large, random sample of the population aged 16 and over about offences they have experienced over the last year, whether or not these have been reported to the police. The results yield an estimate of the number of different offences in 1987 which can be set against offences recorded by the police. Now that it has been repeated over time, the BCS can help to identify crime trends and see whether or not these are reflecting trends in offences recorded by the police. It can also examine the characteristics of offences that victims experience, and how risks of crime vary for different people. For instance, it can show who is most vulnerable to burglary, what losses and damage are likely to result, and how the victims are emotionally affected.

Crime surveys were developed in the mid-1960s in the United States leading to the establishment in 1972 of the US National Crime Survey, which continues today. Against the background of the US work, national crime surveys have now also been carried out in many other countries: for instance, Canada, Australia, the Netherlands, Israel, Sweden, Switzerland, and the Republic of Ireland. Local level surveys have also been mounted, often to assess the effect of local crime prevention initiatives, which themselves can change the willingness of the public to report offences, or the ease with which they might do this.

In Britain, the first use of crime survey techniques was in a 1966 OPCS survey which asked questions about victimisation (Durant *et al.,* 1972). Since 1972, the General Household Survey has intermittently carried questions on residential burglary (see, eg, Home Office, 1982). An important test of crime survey methods was carried out in London in 1972 (Sparks *et al.,* 1977), and in the wake of this, research on the 'Urban Criminal' included victimisation questions (see, Bottoms *et al.,* 1987), as did a Home Office study comparing victimisation among black and white residents in a Manchester area (Tuck and Southgate, 1981).

The first British Crime Survey (BCS) was carried out in 1982 in England and Wales (Hough and Mayhew, 1983), and Scotland (Chambers and Tombs, 1984). Two years later, a second survey was carried out again in England and Wales (see Hough and Mayhew, 1985). Findings from the two previous surveys have been presented in a large number of publications both by Research and Planning Unit staff and academics working in this country and abroad (the main ones are listed in Appendix H).

The BCS programme also lent impetus to a number of local surveys recently mounted in this country to examine crime in specific areas: for instance, in Nottinghamshire and adjacent counties (Farrington and Dowds, 1985); in Merseyside (Kinsey, 1985); in Islington (Jones *et al.*, 1986); in Hammersmith (Painter *et al.*, 1989); and in Newham (London Borough of Newham, 1987). These surveys have generally adopted BCS methods, and many of its questions.

The BCS and other crime surveys have confirmed that a great many crimes go unrecorded by the police, principally because not all victims report what has happened to them. In general this is because the incident is not seen as sufficiently important, or because calling the police is not thought to provide any remedy (see Chapter 3). Offences which are not reported or recorded make up the so-called 'dark figure' of crime, and the survey has been able to show how the size of this dark figure' varies for different offences. It is larger of course for less serious offences such as vandalism.

Recorded crime statistics remain one of the measures of police workload and how this is distributed across different forces and offence types. They have also been extensively used as a 'barometer' of crime levels and trends, though there is now far greater awareness of their shortcomings for this purpose. The manner and extent of police recording will inevitably reflect variations in 'book-keeping' practices, discretion, and even the numbers of officers available. More importantly, while the police are heavily dependent on victims for information about crime, the fact that not all crimes are reported means that police statistics cannot be comprehensive. The large 'dark figure' for many offences means that any change in the public's propensity to report can alter the number of recorded offences independent of any change in the underlying volume of crime experienced. Variations in recorded crime rates over time or place, then, can reflect the processes by which statistics of recorded crime are compiled, as much as the conditions they are intended to depict.

Many crime surveys have demonstrated how their indices of crime can differ from those based on recorded offences. For example, police statistics suggested a much greater increase in recorded household burglaries between 1972 and 1980 than did the General Household Survey. The United States National Crime Survey shows a decrease in most offences between 1976-1985, whilst the trend in recorded crime from the Uniform Crime Report (UCR) is more static (Bureau of Justice Statistics, 1988). Crime surveys can also give a different picture of crime levels across areas. The 1982 BCS, for example, showed that the extent of crime in Scotland is much on a par with that in England and Wales, though police statistics indicate Scotland is more crime-ridden (see Mayhew and Smith, 1985). The Nottingham survey was mounted to find out why, at the time, the county topped the 'league table' of recorded crime, with rates equal to Merseyside and London. It demonstrated that levels of crime in Nottinghamshire were actually only slightly higher than in adjacent counties, but that its very high recorded crime rates could be largely attributed to distinctive recording practices on the part of the Nottinghamshire police.

Crime surveys do not simply count crimes but collect additional information about the characteristics of crime and its victims. The information systems of the police contain some details about what different offences entail, and draws on evidence from a wider range of people involved (eg, witnesses and suspects) than crime surveys, which are limited to details provided simply by victims themselves (cf. Reiss, 1986). Nevertheless, much of the information available to the police is not routinely recorded, and apart from showing risks across different police force areas, is not developed to show risks against different victims. Police forces are now tending to carry out fuller analysis of their statistics, and much work has been done recently by the Home Office Statistical Department eg: see Home Office (1986). But the fact remains that crime surveys – at least for the offences they cover - offer more flexibility in the construction of measures of risk, and a fuller picture of what different offences are typically like. As an additional feature, the large sample of respondents needed to estimate victimisation risks reliably can be asked about a variety of other crime-related issues. In the 1988 BCS, some of the questions put to respondents were about Neighbourhood Watch schemes, contacts with the police, and fear of crime (Appendix C gives full details of the coverage of the 1988 BCS).

The scope of crime surveys

What exactly is it that crime surveys set out to count, and how well do they do it? The crime counted by the BCS and by the police is different. The survey, of course, deals with unreported as well as reported offences. It covers some offences - common assaults and threats - which are not included in the 'notifiable offences' series used by the police and the Home Office. And it is confined to counting crimes against clearly identifiable individual victims and their property. It does not cover crimes for which an organisation is the victim: eg, fraud, shoplifting, or fare evasion (which are hard to measure); nor commercial burglary and robbery. Nor does it count offences involving drug and alcohol abuse, consensual sexual offences, or crimes where people may not have been aware that they have been victimised, as in an assortment of frauds. Also omitted are crimes committed against children (the lower age limit in the BCS was 16), and offences that damage a diffuse population, such as violations of industrial safety codes.

But differences in coverage apart, there is a more basic conceptual problem of how far the definitions of crime of the survey, the public, and the police match. Neither the BCS nor police records can measure what the public defines as 'crime' - if indeed any consistent popular definition exists. Actions which many people will definitely regard as crimes are not represented in the BCS (eg, consumer fraud); and some incidents treated as offences within the survey might be on the borderline of what ordinary members of the public would regard as 'criminal' (eg, fights after closing time). The BCS definition of crime is arrived at by collecting information from victims on incidents within the survey's coverage which are technically criminal, and *post hoc* the surveyors decide how the incident is to be classified. Close attention is paid to legal criteria in classification, and procedures deliberately mirror those followed by the police. But there will be some differences.

First, the police judge whether complainants have given an accurate and truthful account and whether there is evidence that an offence has actually occurred; in contrast, the BCS takes what a respondent says more at face value. Secondly, the BCS applies no threshold of severity; any incident that is technically a crime is counted (or, more or less: some 7% of incidents in the 1988 BCS were excluded because no apparent crime had been committed, or the incident fell outside the categories.) Thus, the survey applies what might be called a *nominal* definition of crime: a count of actions which according to the letter of the law *could* be punished, regardless perhaps of the value of doing so, and regardless in all cases of whether the layman would really see the incident as a 'crime' as such.

The police use a more 'operational' definition of crime. They count incidents reported by victims which are seen as crimes as (i) defined by the criminal law (ie, which *could* be punished by a court); (ii) which *should* merit the attention of the criminal justice system; and (iii) which meet organisational demands for reasonable evidence. For many offences, public and police definitons will coincide. Burglaries and car thefts, for instance, will clearly be regarded by respondents as a breach of the law, even if they do not always think it worthwhile bringing in the system in their particular case; and the police themselves would be unlikely to leave such incidents unrecorded. Other offences – scuffles in clubs, minor criminal damage, some types of domestic trouble – while technically criminal, may be left unreported; or when the police are called in they might be left unrecorded either because formal action is seen as inappropriate, or because weak evidence lead them to 'no-crime' the incident for statistical purposes. The count of recorded crime reflects the judgements made by police and public along the line. The scale of attrition at the various stages is difficult to pinpoint precisely, and it will vary for different offences. In any event, the definitional agreement between the public and the police will be weakest for less serious incidents, those about which moral consensus is weak, and those where the legal criteria for taking action is marginal. On balance, the BCS will count a broader and more value-free set of incidents than police statistics - and indeed it has to if the survey is to be able to detect shifts in reporting and recording practices over time.

To set against this overcounting, however, there is undoubtedly much undercounting of crime in the BCS simply because of the survey process. This is discussed below. And it is not the case, as some might imagine, that the extra crimes which surveys count are necessarily offences which 'are not worth worrying about'. The 1984 survey showed that while the majority of unreported incidents were judged not to be serious or amenable to effective police action, a good number were rated as serious. Conversely, many incidents which *were* reported were thought to be relatively trivial and not the type to deserve much police attention (see Pease, 1988). These last offences will comprise a good proportion of recorded offences.

Survey methodology has various technical limitations which bear on the second question of how well the BCS counts what it sets out to. (For extended discussion of these limitations, see Sparks, 1982; Block and Block, 1984; and Skogan, 1986). In the first place, like any sample survey, the BCS faces problems of adequately representing the total population. To be consistent with earlier sweeps, the 1988 BCS used the Electoral Register as its sampling frame, which is not ideal. Groups which are under-represented on voting registers (eg, ethnic minorities, the young, and the less socially stable) may be particularly vulnerable to victimisation, as may those in institutions, who are not covered in the survey. As in any survey, a proportion of selected respondents will always be impossible to locate and others will refuse to be interviewed. Though the 1988 BCS achieved a good response rate of 77%, non-respondents may, like those omitted from the sampling frame, include a disproportionately high number of victims. Even when respondents are actually interviewed, interviewers sometimes make mistakes, misread questions, lead or mislead respondents and lose questionnaires. And, of course, crime surveys question only a sample of the population and error may arise because of this. The BCS sample is large by the standards of most surveys, but errors arising from the sampling procedure are still large, in particular for rare crimes, such as robbery or rape. Bearing in mind sampling error, some categories of crime which are exceptionally well-reported to the police (for instance, theft of vehicles, and high-value burglaries) are probably counted more accurately by police statistics. (Estimates of sampling errors are provided in Appendix D.)

There is also a set of more specific limitations which arise from the difficulty of the task facing respondents. When a respondent is asked about their experience of crime, many things can stand in the way of accurate answers. The respondent may:

* simply forget a relevant incident (or be ignorant of it);
* remember the incident, but think it happened before the reference period;
* remember an earlier incident as happening within the reference period;
* remember a relevant incident but not be prepared to mention it;
* fail to realise that an incident meets the terms of the question; or even
* make an offence up.

Methodological work shows that these factors work, on balance, to undercount survey-defined offences. In general, minor offences such as low-value thefts and acts of vandalism are readily forgettable, and are particularly likely to remain hidden when people are asked to recall incidents occurring over a relatively long period (an average of 14 months in the BCS). Crimes where victim and offender are acquainted are also less likely than others to be reported at interview: people may not think of these as 'real crimes' and, especially in cases of domestic violence, may be reticent with the interviewer. *There is little doubt that BCS counts of sexual offences and domestic or non-stranger violence are underestimates.*

As well as many crimes not being recalled or reported to interviewers, there may also be differences in recall between groups of respondents. For example, some offences, particularly assaults, are more often reported by better educated respondents, though it seems unlikely they are really more at risk. The most likely explanation is that they are able to complete survey questionnaires better, and for some offences may have a lower threshold of what is 'crime'. Methodological work has not been able to quantify the 'education effect' precisely, but Gottfredson (1988), in reviewing the evidence, argues that it does not seriously jeopardise the relationship between risks and other demographic factors.

These limitations by no means vitiate survey-based indices of crime. Many of the biassing factors should be fairly constant over time: a population's preparedness to report crimes to the police may well change over the period of a decade, but ability to perform the memory tasks demanded in a BCS interview should remain more static. Moreover, the value of crime surveys should be assessed not against the yardstick of perfection, but against the existing alternatives: survey and police statistics combined enable the contours of crime to be mapped far better than police statistics alone.

The design of the 1988 British Crime Survey

Fieldwork for the third BCS was carried out in early 1988. A contract for fieldwork and data preparation was awarded jointly to Social and Community Planning Research (who conducted the first sweep) and NOP Market Research (who conducted the second). As in the 1982 survey, the Scottish Home and Health Department extended the survey to a sample of 5,000 in Scotland (results for Scotland are not covered in this report). For England and Wales, the survey's design and development was undertaken by the Home Office Research and Planning Unit in collaboration with SCPR and NOP. The Research and Planning Unit has been solely responsible for analysis of the data and preparation of reports on results for England and Wales.

A departure for the 1988 survey was coverage of two separate samples. The first was a 'core' sample, which as in previous sweeps was designed to be nationally representative of people aged 16 or older. One adult in each of 10,392 households in England and Wales was interviewed. The second was an ethnic minority 'booster' sample of some 1,349 Afro-Caribbeans (West Indians and Africans) and Asians (Indians, Pakistanis and Bangladeshis). This sample was taken to examine victimisation risks among ethnic minorities, and their attitudes to and experiences of the police. (Some results on ethnic minority risks are given in Chapter 5.)

To maintain consistency with previous sweeps, respondents in the core sample were selected using the Electoral Register as a sampling frame; interviews were conducted in 77% of eligible households. The 'booster' sample was selected through a rather different procedure, and the response rate for this sample was 60%. Further information about the selection of the samples and the survey's design is presented in Appendix C.

All respondents answered a *Main Questionnaire.* This included some attitudinal questions and then 'screened' people to see if they or other members of their household had been the victim of crime. The large number of 'screening' questions are couched in everyday language rather than using legal terms: eg in the last . . . months, has anyone got into your home without permission, in order to steal? Anyone giving a positive answer then completes a supplementary questionnaire about the incident, on the basis of which an offence classification is made. Respondents were asked about their own experience and that of others in the household for *household crimes*: burglary, thefts of and from vehicles, vandalism, and theft from the home. They were asked only about their own experience with respect to *personal crimes*: assaults, robberies, thefts from the person, sexual offences, and other personal thefts. This distinction reflects the fact that for some crimes, such as burglary, the household is a natural unit of analysis, whereas for others the individual is a better choice. At the request of the Health and Safety Executive, a new 'screener' question was added to the 1988 survey on respondents' experience of being verbally abused at work by members of the public with whom they came into contact in their work (for some results see Chapter 4).

Details of each incident revealed by the screen questions were collected on *Victim Forms* (up to a limit of four incidents). All respondents completed one or other of two versions of a *Follow-Up* questionnaire. The first covered questions principally about security behaviour in relation to burglary and autocrime, and Neighbourhood watch. The second covered the public's contacts with, and attitudes to the police; all booster sample respondents completed this *Follow-up* questionnaire. Personal details were collected from all respondents in a *Demographic Questionnaire.*

The structure of this report

This report does not cover all the results from the 1988 BCS, but summarises some of its key findings. It will be followed by a number of more detailed papers on specific topics. Chapter 2 covers the extent of crime in 1987, providing estimates of unreported and unrecorded crime; it also examines changes in crime from 1981 and 1983. Chapter 3 looks in more detail at reporting to the police, examining reasons given for not reporting, and how victims felt the police had handled their report. Chapter 4 looks at victimisation at work. Chapter 5 examines risks of crime among Afro-Caribbeans and Asians. Chapter 6 examines results about Neighbourhood Watch schemes: who are most likely to be members, what they do, and how they have been affected. The findings of Chapters 2–6 are summarised at the end of each chapter. The concluding chapter (Chapter 7) draws out the most important new findings from the survey and discusses their implications. Additional tables of results are provided in Appendices A and B. Details of the survey design are presented in Appendix C. A technical note on sampling error is included in Appendix D. Appendix E describes how the comparison was made between BCS figures and crimes recorded by the police; Appendix F gives details about the comparison of findings on burglary from the General Household Survey and the BCS; Appendix G describes the ACORN system of area classification. A bibliography of BCS reports is included as Appendix H.

2 The extent of crime

The British Crime Survey yields estimates of the extent of various crimes including those unreported to the police. It covers violence against the person, and theft of, and damage to, private property.[1] Results from the 1988 survey can be set against those from the two previous sweeps. Respondents describe the offences they have experienced in the preceding year, so the results of the three surveys cover crime in 1981, 1983 and 1987.

Figure 1 shows which offences were most common in 1987. (As do statistics of recorded offences, some offences include attempts.) The estimates have been derived by applying rates from the 'core' sample to the household and adult populations in England and Wales. (Table A.1, Appendix A gives the rates on which numbers of incidents are based.) It should be said that as the estimates are derived from a sample they are subject to sampling error. For instance, the survey's 'best estimate' of the number of incidents of burglary in 1987 is 1,180,000; with 95% certainty the number falls between 1,334,000 and 1,025,000.

As was shown in previous surveys, the vast majority of offences are against property. Motor vehicles (cars, vans, motorcycles and mopeds) emerge as a strikingly common targets: nearly a third of all incidents uncovered by the BCS involved theft of, theft from, or damage to cars, vans or motorcycles. In contrast, burglaries formed a relatively small proportion of survey crimes, at just under 9%. In most incidents involving theft, losses were relatively low – under £50 in 70% of incidents.

Violent offences (wounding, robbery and sexual offences) comprised 6% of BCS crime; another 11% were less serious common assaults which are not recorded as notifiable offences by the police (see below). Most assaults and crimes of violence did not result in any serious physical injury; in 15% of cases did the victim need any sort of professional medical attention, and in 1% of cases the victim was admitted to hospital. Victim and offender were unknown to each other in about half of cases; 18% of incidents involved family, lovers or ex-lovers – though as discussed in Chapter 1, the BCS will undercounnt domestic violence. Without doubt, too, the number of sexual offences will also be an underestimate, particularly offences committed by non-strangers. In all, only some 15 sexual offences were uncovered by the survey among nearly 5,500 women – though as mentioned in chapter 1 this is likely to be an underestimate of the real extent of sexual victimisation.

---

[1] The BCS questionnaire also deals with doorstep thefts of milk bottles and threatening behaviour. Doorstep thefts are not included in analyses in the present report, though they are frequent: some one in 12 households said they had milk stolen at least once over about 14 months. Threats are not counted as BCS offences in this chapter as few meet the criteria of a notifiable or non-notifiable offences. In other chapters, threats are covered where specified.

Figure 1

British Crime Survey estimates of certain offences in England and Wales, 1987.

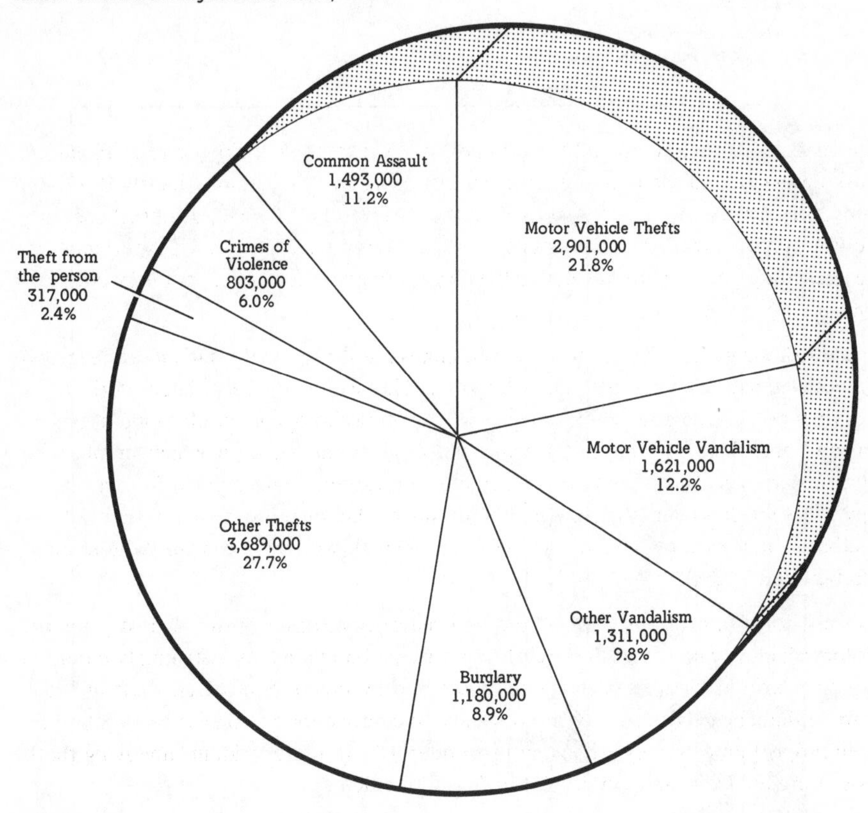

Note :

'Crimes of Violence' comprise wounding, robbery and sexual offences. (Unlike common assault these are all 'notifiable' offences.) 'Motor vehicle thefts' included attempted thefts. 'Other thefts' comprise personal thefts not involving contact with an offender, together with thefts in a dwelling, bicycle thefts and other household thefts not involving vehicles.

Reporting and recording of crimes

By combining information from the BCS with police statistics, estimates can be derived of the proportion of crimes reported to, and recorded by, the police. This can only be done, however, for a subset of crime types (see Appendix E for further details).[2] For crime categories which can be compared, Figure 2 shows unreported incidents, those which were reported but not recorded, and those which found their way into police records (see also Table A.2 in Appendix A).

[2] For example, no comparison is possible for shoplifting or fraud because the survey cannot identify most of these offences. Nor are there any survey figures conparable with 'other thefts' in Criminal Statistics since these include a wider miscellany of offences than picked up in the survey.

Figure 2

Levels of recorded and unrecorded crime, 1987:
British Crime Survey estimates

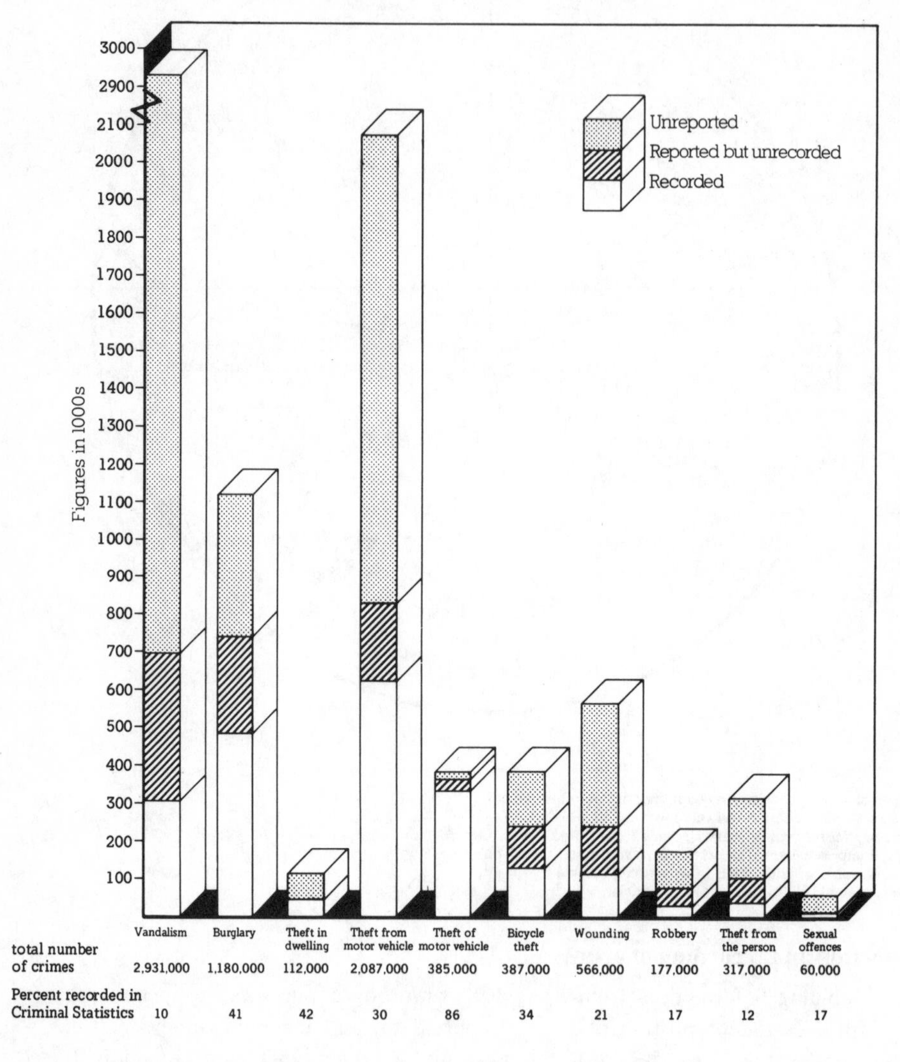

	Vandalism	Burglary	Theft in dwelling	Theft from motor vehicle	Theft of motor vehicle	Bicycle theft	Wounding	Robbery	Theft from the person	Sexual offences
total number of crimes	2,931,000	1,180,000	112,000	2,087,000	385,000	387,000	566,000	177,000	317,000	60,000
Percent recorded in Criminal Statistics	10	41	42	30	86	34	21	17	12	17

Note:

The figures for the total number of crimes are best estimates from BCS results grossed up to the population of England and Wales, and rounded. Recorded crime in each category is derived from *Criminal Statistics, 1987* of notifiable offences recorded by the police, adjusted to maximise comparability with survey data. (see Appendix E).

It can be seen that a large proportion of incidents went unreported for all categories of crime except vehicle theft, which was well-reported. The overall reporting rate for crimes shown in Figure 2 was 37%. Low reporting rates emerged for vandalism, theft in a dwelling, other household thefts, and the small number of sexual offences uncovered by the survey - about a fifth to a quarter of incidents came to police notice. About 30% of incidents were reported of personal thefts and thefts from the person (the latter involving some contact between victim and offenders, but no violence or threat). About 40% of woundings and robberies were reported, and about the same proportion of thefts from motor vehicles. Bicycle thefts and burglaries were more often reported (about two-thirds were). Burglaries with loss were much more frequently reported (86% were) than no-loss incidents (44%). How far 1988 reporting rates have changed since the two earlier surveys is taken up later. The reasons why crimes are not reported are examined in Chapter 3.

Figure 2 (and Table A.2 of Appendix A) shows that many of the offences reported to the police do not get recorded as crimes - or are not recorded, in the crime categories shown. Overall, for instance, the police would appear to record about two-thirds of the property crimes known to them. BCS estimates of the 'recording shortfall' are not precise. This is both because of sampling error in the survey estimates and because of the difficulties in comparing like with like when matching BCS offence classifications with those used by the police (though in principle the same rules are adhered to). However, the three surveys have yielded broadly similar estimates, and there can be little doubt that many reported incidents are not recorded in the crime categories suggested by victims' descriptions.

One likely reason for the shortfall is that the police do not accept victims' accounts of incidents; they may - quite rightly - think that a report of an incident is mistaken or disingenuous, or may feel that there is simply insufficient evidence to say that a crime has been committed. Some incidents *will* have been recorded, of course, but in different crime categories – where, for example, it is indisputable that criminal damage has been committed, a burglary may have been attempted. In addition a repeated crime (by which one person commits many offences over a period with a common modus operandi) may be counted by the police as one offence; but to the victim and hence the BCS, each would have the same chance of being reported. Some incidents may have been regarded as too trivial to warrant formal police action - particularly if complainants indicated they wanted the matter dropped or were unlikely to give evidence, or if the incident had already been satisfactorily resolved.[3]

In sum, there is a considerable gap between survey estimates and figures of offences recorded by the police both because many crimes go unreported and because the police

[3] Thefts in a dwelling show no 'shortfall': the number recorded by e police is larger than the number estimated by the survey to have been reported. The same result emerged from the 1984 survey. As well as sampling error, the discrepancy may be accounted for by differences in classification: some of the incidents which the BCS would classify as burglary may have been judged by the police to be the lesser offence of theft in a dwelling, perhaps because there was insufficient evidence of trespass.

do not record all the offences about which they are informed. Reported offences which fall by the wayside in the police recording process may not be especially serious, but there is no way of finding out their characteristics from the survey. The 1984 BCS, however, was able to show differences between offences reported to the police and those not. Victims' assessments of the seriousness of what happened was an important factor in reporting, though not such as to indicate that all and only serious crime come to be represented in recorded offences. A substantial minority of *unreported* crimes were serious - in terms of subjective ratings by victims of injury and material loss. And many BCS incidents regarded as trivial and undeserving of police priority were nonetheless reported.[4]

The numbers of crimes in 1981, 1983 and 1987

Table 1 shows the estimated number of crimes in 1981, 1983 and 1987 falling within the survey's coverage.[5] As the estimates are subject to sampling error, many *apparent* changes over time are not statistically significant. Rates of crime in the three years are shown in Table A.1, Appendix A.[6]

[4] Victims were asked to rate the seriousness of what had happened to them on a 20-point scale. They were also asked what priority the police should give to solving crimes like theirs (see Hough and Mayhew (1985) and Pease (1988)).

[5] The figures for 1981 and 1983 in Table 1 and some other tables differ slightly than those previously published. This is because some incidents from earlier surveys were reclassified to maximise consistency of offence classification across the three surveys.

[6] Comparisons of BCS trends based on the number of offences give a steeper increase in crime than on the basis of rates per 10,000 persons or per 10,000 households, as the number of adults and households in Engand and Wales has increased. There was a 3.6% increase in the number of adults between 1981 and 1987 and a 4.5% increase in households. As household numbers have increased more than population, using rates to estimate the number of offences will produce a slightly steeper increases in household offences than personal ones.

Table 1

Offences in England and Wales,1981, 1983 and 1987: British Crime Survey estimates

Figures in 000's	*1981*	*1983*	*1987*	*% change 1983-87*	*% change 1981-87*
HOUSEHOLD OFFENCES					
1. Vandalism	2,695	2,774	2,931	6	9
2. Burglary	744	907	1,180	30**	59**
Attempts and no loss	373	457	665	46**	78*
With loss	371	450	515	14	39**
3. Theft in a dwelling	147	129	112	-13	-24
4. Theft from motor vehicle	1,277	1,525	2,087	37**	63**
5. Theft of motor vehicle	284	282	385	37**	36**
6. Bicycle theft	215	286	387	35	80**
7. Other household theft	1,537	1,693	1,823	8	19
PERSONAL OFFENCES					
8. Sexual offences	30	65	60	[-8	100]
9. Common assault	1,402	1,429	1,493	4	6
10. Wounding	507	423	566	34	12
11. Robbery	163	145	177	22	9
12. Theft from the person	434	505	317	[-37	-27]
13. Other personal thefts	1,588	1,730	1,794	4	13
All household offences (1-7)	6,898	7,599	8,885	17**	29**
All personal offences (8-13)	4,123	4,297	4,407	3	7

Notes:

1 BCS estimates of the number of crimes has been derived by applying rates to the household and adult (aged 16 or more) population of England and in Wales in each of the years. The numbers are 'best estimates' only. Because of rounding, sub-totals do not always add to totals.

2 The statistical significance of the changes between years is calculated on the basis of rates to take population changes into account. Double-starred differences are significant at the 5% level (two-tail test, taking complex standard error into account). This means that the chances are less than 1 in 20 that the change has occurred simply through sampling error. Single-starred differences are significant at the 10% level.

3 The increase in sexual offences after 1981 is due to questionnaire changes. The drop in theft from the person in 1987 is due classification changes.

4 Best estimates for 1981 and 1983 are slightly different from those published before mainly on account of updated household and adult population figures.

5 Categories 2, 7, 8, 9, 11, 12 and 13 include attempts.

6 Weighted data. Source: 1982, 1984 and 1988 (core sample) BCS.

Household offences

Household offences as a whole increased more steeply than personal offences: there were 17% more in 1987 than 1983, and 29% more than in 1981 - both statistically significant increases. Looking at individual offence categories, the increase in burglaries with loss was only statistically significant over the longer 1981-87 period, reflecting the steeper rise between 1981-83 than thereafter. Attempted burglaries have risen more than loss burglaries, and this may reflect better security on the part of householders making it more difficult for burglars to gain entry. The trend in burglary is complex and is further discussed.

The increase in *motor vehicle* crime could partly reflect more cars on the road, though a more likely factor contributing to thefts from cars may be more and better audio equipment. The increase in risks for vehicle *owners* in 1987 was rather less steep - as the number of owners has increased more than households since the earlier surveys. (Table A.3 in Appendix A shows rates of vehicle crime based on owners only.) Among owners, the risk of having their car stolen increased, but not to a statistically significant degree. Thefts from vehicles, however, increased significantly, as did attempted thefts. Vandalism to vehicles was significantly lower than in 1983. Overall, risks posed by vehicle crime were high in 1987:

* 22% of owners were the target at least once of some form of vehicle crime;
* 8% experienced at least one incident of vandalism;
* 12% had something stolen off or from their vehicles at least once; and
* 2.5% of owners had their cars driven away.

Increased bicycle ownership may again be behind some of the large rise in steep increase in theft numbers of *bicycle thefts* (up 80% since 1981). However, the particularly steep increase in thefts between 1981 and 1983 was thought to be due to the vogue for 'BMX' bikes, and since then the increasing popularity and value of mountain bikes etc may have made bikes a continuingly attractive target for theft.

There were no significant changes over time in the number of incidents of vandalism, theft in a dwelling or other household theft offences.

Personal offences

Since 1981 there has been only a 7% increase in personal offences, and a 3% increase since 1983. The drop in theft from the person in 1987 is artefactual, due to a change in rules for classifying the offence. The higher figures for sexual offences in 1983 and 1987 also reflect changes to the questions about sexual victimisation. These were made to reduce the evident reticence of such victims to mention incidents to interviewers.

Annual average increases in crime

Where crime has risen, it has done so less steeply since 1983 than it did between 1981 and 1983 (see Table A.4 in Appendix A). For instance, household offences as a whole rose by 5% a year between 1981 and 1983, and by 4% a year thereafter. Personal offences rose by 2.1% a year in the earlier period and by less than 1% between 1983 and 1987.

Changes in crime between 1981 and 1987: BCS and recorded offences

Do recorded crime figures show a similar pattern of change to that identified by the BCS? Table 2 compares the change in BCS offences over the three surveys with that in offences recorded by the police. Necessarily it compares subsets of both BCS and police categories, and sexual offences and thefts from the person are omitted because of classification changes which have upset the BCS trend.

Generally there has been a flatter rise in BCS estimates of crime than in recorded offences. Over the six-year period from 1981-1987 the divergence between BCS estimates and recorded offences is statistically significant: BCS crime has risen by 30% as against a 41% rise in recorded offences. Between 1983 and 1987, the divergence was too small to reach statistical significance (recorded offences rose by 26% and BCS figures by 21%).

Table 2

A comparison between the British Crime Survey and notifiable offences recorded by the police

Figures in 000s	*1987 Police*	*1987 BCS*	*% re-corded*	*% change 1983-7 Police*	*% change 1983-7 BCS*	*% change 1981-7 Police*	*% change 1981-7 BCS*
Vandalism	305	2931	10	33	6**	52	9**
Burglary	483	1180	41	12	30*	38	59
Attempts and no loss	107	665	16	19	46*	46	78*
With loss	376	515	73	10	14	36	39
Theft in a dwelling	47	112	42	-2	-13	0	-24
Theft from motor vehicle	626	2087	30	55	37**	74	63
Theft of motor vehicles	333	385	86	20	37	17	36
Bicycle theft	133	387	34	-8	35**	5	80**
Wounding	118	566	21	26	34	40	12
Robbery	30	177	17	49	22	62	9
Wounding & robbery	147	743	20	30	31	44	11*
TOTAL	2073	7810	27	26	21	41	30*

Notes:

1 Totals do not sum sub-totals because of rounding.

2 Double-asterisked divergences between police and BCS figures are significant at the 5% level (two-tail test, taking complex standard error into account). Single-asterisked divergences are significant at the 10% level.

3 Offences recorded by the police have been adjusted slightly to improve comparability with the BCS (see Appendix E for details).

4 Weighted data. Source: 1982, 1984 and 1988 (core sample) BCS. See Home Office, (1988)

Changes in reporting to the police will help explain why BCS estimates differ from police figures. (If more offences are reported, more will find their way into police records, thereby inflating the increase in recorded crime relative to that shown by the BCS.) For the subset of crimes comparable with offences recorded by the police, there has been a statistically significant increase of 15% in reporting since 1981. Since 1983, reporting has risen by 4% (not statistically significant). Table 3 shows reporting trends over successive BCS sweeps.

Table 3

Percent of BCS offences reported to the police, 1981, 1983 and1987

	% reported			Difference in % rate of reporting	Difference in % rate of reporting
	1981	*1983*	*1987*	*1983-87*	*1981-7*
HOUSEHOLD OFFENCES					
1 Vandalism	22.2	22.0	23.7	8	7
2 Burglary	66.2	67.9	63.2	-8	-5
Attempts and no loss	48.4	50.2	43.7	-13	-10
With loss	84.7	86.6	86.3	0	2
3 Theft in a dwelling	19.3	25.8	17.1	-34	-11
4 Theft from motor vehicle	30.3	38.2	39.9	4	32**
5 Theft of motor vehicle	94.9	96.4	94.9	-2	0
6 Bicycle theft	63.9	68.2	62.4	-9	-2
7 Other household theft	26.5	20.9	26.0	24*	-2
All household offences	33.4	34.6	38.0	10**	14**
PERSONAL OFFENCES					
8 Sexual offences	28.3	8.1	20.8	[157]	[-27]
9 Common assault	25.1	30.5	32.5	7	29
10 Wounding	40.2	59.6	43.3	-27	8
11 Robbery	46.5	39.0	43.9	13	-6
12 Theft from the person	31.3	31.2	33.6	8	7
13 Other personal theft	27.1	29.8	31.2	5	37**
All personal offences	27.1	33.1	33.7	2	24**
ALL BCS OFFENCES	31.1	34.1	36.6	7*	18**
COMPARABLE WITH CRIMINAL STATISTICS					
Household (1-6)	35.4	38.4	41.1	7	16**
Personal (10-11)	41.7	54.3	43.4	-20	4
Total	36.0	39.8	41.3	4	15**

Notes:

1. Question: 'Did the police come to know about the matter?' The table includes incidents which occurred in the full recall period, not the calendar year.
2. Double-starred differences are significant at the 5% level (2-tail test taking complex standard error into account). Differences are based on unrounded figures.
3. Reporting figures for sexual offences are unreliable because of small numbers.
4. Weighted data (unweighted n=5023, 1987). Source: BCS 1982, 1984 and 1987 (core sample)

For which specific offences is the movement in recorded offences matched or contradicted by BCS estimates? Where trends diverge, this may be explained by reporting changes, or changes in the extent and manner of recording by the police of offences reported to them. Estimates of the proportion of reported offences which are recorded should, as said, be regarded cautiously, but some mention is made below of them. (Table A.5 in Appendix A summarises changes between 1981 and 1987 in 'best' estimates of the percentage of reported offences which are recorded, and the percentage of *all* BCS offences which are recorded.)

Offences are singled out below (and in Table A.5, Appendix A) for which there has been a statistically significant divergence between BCS figures and recorded offences (for simplicity, 'police figures'). In summary, police figures have risen *more* than the BCS for vandalism, thefts from motor vehicles, and violent offences. For bicycle theft and burglary, the opposite is the case.

For *vandalism*, the sharper increase in police figures than in BCS estimates holds both for 1983-87 (police rise 33%, BCS rise 6%), and for 1981-87 (police rise 52%, BCS rise 9%). Across the same years there has been a rise in the propensity to report vandalism incidents, and there is evidence that the level at which reported crimes are recorded has also increased. It may also be that the sharper rise in vandalism recorded by the police reflects an increasing tendency against classifying incidents as attempted burglary where the evidence is doubtful.

There has also been a sharper increase in police figures for *thefts from motor vehicles* between 1983-87 than in the BCS. There was a large increase in reporting these offences between 1981-87, though between 1983-87 the increase in reporting was not marked.

Although the divergence between BCS and police trends for *wounding* and *robbery* do not reach the level of statistical significance when considered separately, taken together there has been a much flatter increase between 1981-87 in BCS estimates (11%) than in police figures (44%) – and this is unlikely to be explained by sampling error.[7] The increase in reporting of wounding and robbery to the police is not large (4%), but there is some evidence that there has been an increase in the number of reported offences recorded by the police.

However, interpretation of the divergence between BCS and police figures is made more complex by the fact that the dividing line between 'wounding' and 'common assault' is often difficult to draw both for the BCS and, no doubt, the police. For common assaults (not shown in Table 2 as they are not notifiable offences), BCS figures show a fairly flat

[7] The figures for wounding and robbery since 1983 are *on the face of it* less encouraging. This reflects the fact that, for both wounding and robbery, BCS figures were lower in 1983 than in 1981, and thus the 1983-87 increase was greater than over the six-year period. However, both of the falls in 1983 could have been due to sampling error. They could also have reflected changes in how offences were classified; the classification of wounding and robbery was probably more comparable between 1981 and 1987.

trend: these less serious, though numerically more important assaults, have increased by only 6% since 1981, though reporting to the police has risen sharply. Even a modest increase in the reporting of such a large category of offences, if accompanied by a tendency by the police to classify more of these as 'wounding', would help explain the rise in recorded 'woundings'. Taking the most reliable inclusive BCS coverage of 'violence' (wounding, robbery, *and* common assault), BCs results do not indicate any large increase in violence: since 1981, these offences have increased modestly, by 8%.

The marked increase in *bicycle theft* since 1981 according to the BCS (up by 80%), contrasts with only a small (5%) increase in police figures. There has been a recent fall in the reporting of bike thefts, which would in part account for the pattern in police figures. The data also suggest that fewer reported bike thefts are recorded by the police, or at least in the bike theft category. The fall in reporting has been among both victims with and without insurance cover, though insurance factors may nonetheless be implicated. Insurance companies have become increasingly inclined to ask for separate cover for bikes, with the likely result that fewer bike owners will have cover and thereby bring in the police for insurance reasons if their bike is stolen. The latest BCS data support this in showing a drop in the proportion of victims with insurance cover for bike theft.

Burglary has also risen significantly *more* according to the BCS than it has in police figures. The BCS rise between 1981-87 was 59%; the police rise 38%. However, *burglaries with loss* have not diverged over the period in a way that cannot be explained by sampling error (the BCS rise was 39%, the police rise 36%). The divergence for 'burglary' as a whole comes mainly from offences recorded as *attempts and no loss*: these have risen more since 1981 than police figures suggest.

Table 3 shows that over the same period there has been a *drop* in the propensity to report burglary particularly attempts (reporting of these is down by 10%). (The drop in reporting was particularly noticeable among victims without insurance cover.) There is also some evidence of a fall in the recording of reported burglaries (some 65% of the number of burglaries estimated to have been reported by the BCS were recorded in 1987 as against 71% in 1981.) Matching police figures on attempted burglaries with those from the BCS is rather difficult, but the data also suggests slightly lower recording of attempted burglaries which are reported.

The remainder of this chapter examines, first, why reporting may have generally increased since 1982. It then turns back to burglary for which, using results from the BCS and the General Household Survey, a survey comparison is available with recorded crime over a 15-year period.

Changes in reporting

As mentioned, 1984 BCS data shows that the decision of victims to report to the police centres largely, though not entirely, on the seriousness of what has happened to them. Overlying seriousness will be a calculation of the personal costs and benefits of reporting, and of the chances that notifying the police will achieve something. Thus, the reasons given by 1984 victims who *did* report (victims were not asked why they reported in 1988) – stressed mainly (i) the personal advantages of doing so (eg, getting property recovered, reducing the risk of further victimisatim, getting police help, and insurance requirements), and (ii) the feeling that there was a social obligation on victims to notify the police (see Hough and Mayhew, 1985: 20-21)). Reasons for *not* reporting given by respondents in the 1988 survey are taken up in Chapter 3, but in brief they primarly reflect judgments that the incident was too minor, or that there was little chance of any satisfactory outcome in terms, for instance, of getting property back, or offenders caught.

There is no way of saying for certain why reporting to the police has generally gone up over the decade. The present data does not suggest that the offences experienced are more serious in terms, for instance, of injury, or time off work; average losses were a little higher, but inflation could account for this. It may be that increased public sensitivity to crime has contributed to higher reporting (because of crime prevention activities such as Neighborhood Watch schemes, for instance), or even less tolerant attitudes towards anti-social behaviour. Quite possibly though, it has became easier to report as more people have a telephone at home, and better access to public phones in working order. Higher owner-occupation may also be implicated since owners are much more inclined to take out insurance.[8]

Whether more people now report because of increased confidence in the police seems on balance unlikely, given that personal advantage and social obligation are the main reasons for reporting. Also, the BCS provides no evidence that attitudes to general police performance have improved either among reporters or non-reporters. The vast majority of people still feel that the police are performing well (75% said they did a good or fair job in their local area). But this assessment is only the same as in 1982, and lower than in 1984 (83%).[9]

Burglary 1972-1987

Since 1972, the General Household Survey (GHS) has intermittently included a question on household burglary. Combining its results with those from the BCS allows a relatively long-term comparison to be made with recorded offences – though the

[8] Telephone ownership has increased within the UK frm 76% of households having a phone in 1981 to 83% in 1987. British Telecom have continued to introduce design changes to public kiosks and have made more phonecard installations as it is thought that these are more reliable. Some 54% of households were owner-occupiers in 1981 (GB), as against 63% in 1987 (GHS figures).

[9] The percentages of those who said they were 'very satisfied' were 35% in 1982, 31% in 1984, and 22% in 1988. A series of polls by MORI since 1981 has also produced, using a slightly different question, evidence of decline in satisfaction with the Police (*News of the World*, 9 April 1989).

soundest comparison has to be restricted to incidents in which a burglar entered the home and stole something (ie, burglaries with loss). Figure 3 shows results. (Appendix F gives further details of the comparison.) Combined GHS/BCS survey estimates have risen by 17% over the 15-year period 1972-87, while recorded offences have increased by 127% – nearly eight times more.[10] The divergence between the two trends varies somewhat according to the particular years compared. It is greater for the earlier part of the period than later: since 1981, for instance, police figures rose only four to five times more than survey measures. Between 1983-87, there is no statistically sound evidence that the trends diverge. Between 1985-1987, survey figures fell – by about 15%. While this drop is not statistically significant, it may nonetheless indicate a fall-off in burglaries with loss, particularly as recorded offences, which remained fairly stable between 1985-87, dropped in 1988 (Home Office, 1989a) . It is not possible to compare GHS and BCS figures on attempted burglary to see whether they peaked around 1985 too. However, as was shown earlier, attempts increased between 1983-87 a good deal more than burglaries with loss.

The long-term increase in recorded burglaries, then, has been substantially steeper than the surveys indicate. Increased reporting will help explain this. Some 78% of burglaries with loss (GHS figures) were reported in 1972 as against nearly 90% in 1987 (BCS figures). Some of the factors influencing this have already been mentioned, but changing patterns of insurance may be particularly important for burglaries with loss. According to the GHS, property stolen in only 19% of burglary incidents was covered by insurance in 1972, whereas the figure was 42% in 1980, and 58% in 1987.

The steeper increase in recorded burglary may also reflect a rise in the proportion of offences reported to the police which are recorded. As explained, estimates cannot be precise, but the 'best guess' is that, in 1972, 59% of reported burglaries were recorded, 67% in 1980, and 85% in 1987. Increasing police manpower, standardisation of recording procedures, and even computerisation may underlie this change. Because proportionately more burglaries are now reported and recorded, the 'dark figure' of burglaries not in police statistics has contracted substantially. The 'best guess' is that 45% of the burglaries committed ended up as recorded offences in 1972 while by 1987 the figure was 73%.

[10] Allowing for sampling error on both the 1972 and 1987 survey figures, one could say with 95% certainty that the survey increase did not exceed 44% ($P<0.05$).

Figure 3

Residential burglaries involving loss, 1972–1988

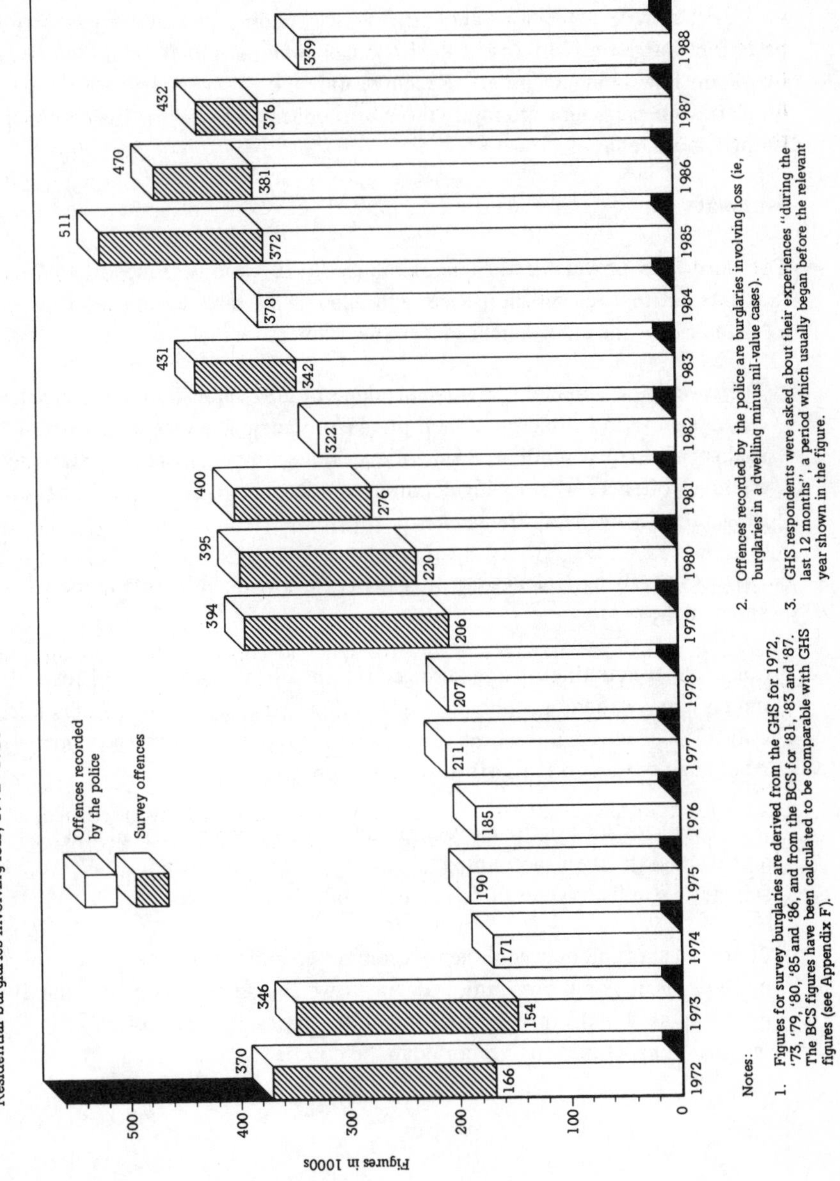

Notes:

1. Figures for survey burglaries are derived from the GHS for 1972, '73, '79, '80, '85 and '86, and from the BCS for '81, '83 and '87. The BCS figures have been calculated to be comparable with GHS figures (see Appendix F).
2. Offences recorded by the police are burglaries involving loss (ie, burglaries in a dwelling minus nil-value cases).
3. GHS respondents were asked about their experiences "during the last 12 months", a period which usually began before the relevant year shown in the figure.

The GHS/BCS results are unique in this country for a long-tem comparison with recorded offences. As the BCS itself is confined to a six-year comparison, conclusions about changes in reporting and recording are inevitably less firm. The survey suggests the most marked contraction of the 'dark figure' (ie, more committed offences ending up in police records) is for vandalism, and wounding and robbery – mirroring the pattern of burglaries with loss over the longer time-period. If anything, fewer bicycle thefts are now being recorded. Recently, too, the same seems to be the case with burglaries, in particular attempts, though a longer time-scale is needed to test these changes more reliably.

Summary

The third BCS provides estimates of the extent of various crimes in 1987, including incidents not reported to the police, and allows 1987 rates to be set against those for 1981 and 1983. The main conclusions of the chapter are:

* There were an estimated 13 million incidents in 1987 falling into the BCS categories of crimes against individuals and their private property. The vast majority were offences against property. Wounding, sexual offences and common assaults comprise only 17% of survey offences. (Excluding common assaults, the figure was 6%). About half of these offences involved strangers.

* Offences involving violence are very heavily outweighed by offences involving theft and damage to property.

* Some under-counting of non-stranger violence in the survey is likely, but present figures show wounding, robbery, sexual offences and common assaults to comprise only 17% of all BCS offences. (Excluding common assaults, the figure was 6%). About half of these offences involved strangers.

* Motor vehicles are a particularly common target for crime: theft of and from vehicles and damage to them accounted for nearly a third of all crime uncovered by the survey. One in five owners faced some sort of vehicle offence in 1987.

* There is a shortfall between offences committed and the number which are recorded by the police. For those crime categories which can be compared, the 1988 BCS revealed, as did the previous surveys, four times as many offences as in police records. Many crimes go unreported to the police.

* There is low reporting to the police of vandalism, thefts of household property, and sexual offences (about three-quarters go unreported). Two-thirds of thefts of personal property and thefts from the person went unreported, and rather more than half of woundings and robberies. A third of burglaries and bicycle thefts were not reported, though most thefts of vehicles were.

* Crime in 1987 was higher than the last survey's figures for 1983, though the rate of increase (21%) is not quite as rapid as that of recorded crime (26%). Compared to 1981 figures from the first survey, the BCS increase in crime (30%) is lower than recorded crime (41%) – a statistically significant difference. This reflects a general increase in reporting to the police. Of BCS offences comparable with police statistics coverage, 41% were reported in 1987, as against 36% in 1981.

* The BCS indicates that the increase in different offences was generally higher between 1981-83 than it was between 1983-87 on an annual average basis. This may indicate some slowing down of risks.

* The most comprehensive BCS estimate of violent crime (wounding, robbery and common assault) shows a relatively modest increase of 8% since 1981.

* Offences which can be reliably said to have risen more in police figures than in the BCS are: vandalism, thefts from motor vehicles, and wounding/robbery.

* Bicycle theft has risen more according to BCS estimates than police figures. A fall in reporting may explain this in part, perhaps reflecting a drop in insurance cover as insurance companies have come to want separate cover for bikes. Changes in recording practices could also be implicated.

* Burglary has also risen more according to BCS estimates, though due principally to an increase in attempted offences – which may indicate that better security is making entry harder for burglars. A drop in reporting may partly explain the divergence between BCS estimates and police statistics, and possibly some recording change.

* Looking at burglaries with loss over a considerably longer period, however, shows that recorded offences have substantially exaggerated the increase in burglary. The BCS and the General Household Survey combined indicate an increase in burglaries 1972 to 1987 in the region of 20%, as against about 125% in police statistics.

* Recorded burglaries suggest a peaking of burglary in 1986, and a downturn since. Survey results are not inconsistent with this for burglaries with loss but the evidence is not conclusive.

3 Reporting to the police

Chapter 2 introduced results from the 1988 survey on reporting to the police, showing an overall increase in reporting since 1981 and considerable variation in the extent to which specific offences were likely to be reported. This chapter focuses first on the reasons why many victims did not bring their offence to the attention of the police. It then turns back to people who *did* report to look at how they notified the police, what response they got, and how satisfied they were with this.

Reasons for not reporting

Victims who had not notified the police most often gave as a reason (they could name more than one) the triviality of the incident; in just under half of unreported crimes victims said the incident involved no loss or damage or was otherwise too trivial to report. In a further fifth of cases victims felt that the police would not have been able to do anything about the incident; in a tenth of cases they felt the offence was not a matter for the police or they dealt with it themselves. Rarely cited was the inconvenience of reporting (2%), dislike of the police (1%), and fear of reprisals (1%). These results are generally ccnsistent with previous findings from the BCS, and with survey results from other countries (see Skogan, 1984).

The reasons for not reporting varied for different types of crime (see Table A.6 in Appendix A). For instance, assaults and thefts in a dwelling were particularly unlikely to be thought a matter for the police. Thefts of personal property – which often take place at work (see chapter 4) – were often reported to someone other than the police. In cases of robbery, theft from the person and theft from vehicles, it was often felt that the police could do nothing.

It is still clear, though, that the major reason for not reporting a crime remains the victims' assessment that it is insufficiently serious to be grist for the mill of formal justice. Non-reporters make a reasonable cost-benefit jugdement, usually deciding not to report when the offence is minor, or when they assume that they will not get their property back, or the offenders will not be caught.

Do decisions not to report reflect confidence in the police? As said, the nature of offence experience is the main determinant of whether victims report, and Chapter 2 suggested that extraneous factors (such as telephone ownership) may be underpinning the general increase in reporting, rather than any change in attitudes to the police. Similarly, previous research has shown that what victims feel about the police has relatively limited significance in non-reporting, and then mainly for the least serious incidents (Skogan, 1984; Hough and Mayhew, 1985).

Comparing the 1988 and 1984 surveys (a comparision with 1982 is difficult because of questionnaire changes), there is no evidence that fear or dislike of the police was a commoner reason for not reporting in 1988 than in 1984. However, people more often mentioned that the police would 'not have bothered or been interested' (see Table 4), and that 'the police could have done nothing'. Taking all BCS offences which went unreported, 32% of victims gave such reasons as against 23% in 1984 ($p<0.01$).[1] The differences were greatest for theft from the person/robbery, bicycle thefts, thefts from motor vehicles, and vandalism. The drop in reporting of attempted and no-loss burglaries remarked on in Chapter 2 does not, in fact, appear to be particularly well explained in terms of victims' expectations about police performance: only slightly more victims in 1988 (28%) gave these 'policing' reasons than in 1984 (24%).

Table 4
Reasons for not reporting associated with the police

	Police could have done nothing		*Police would not bothered*		*Fear/ dislike police*		*Total*	
	1984	*1988*	*1984*	*1988*	*1984*	*1988*	*1984*	*1988*
Vandalism	18	26	9	12	–	–	27	39
Theft from MV	21	30	4	13	–	–	24	43
Burlary	15	17	10	11	1	–	26	27
With loss	12	21	17	6	–	–	28	27
Attempts/no loss	16	16	8	11	–	–	24	28
Bicycle theft	26	19	9	8	–	2	35	29
Other HH theft	15	19	9	12	<1	–	24	31
Assault	6	9	6	4	1	2	12	15
Theft person/robbery	21	30	2	12	1	3	25	45
Other personal thefts	18	17	2	7	1	1	21	25
All offences	16	21	7	10	<1	1	23	32

1. Weighted data. Source: 1984 BCS and 1988 BCS (core sample)

Those who report: how the police came to know

As the police are rarely in a position to discover crime for themselves, reporting behaviour is clearly critical in determining the offences with which the police have to

[1] Non-reporters in 1987 compared with those in earlier surveys may have been more likely to cite these 'police-related' reasons if people with more favourable attitudes to the police have been 'siphoned off' as reporting has increased. Further analysis (for instance, expressing reasons for not reporting on the base of everyone in the sample) shows that this does not explain the pattem of results.

deal. The vast majority of crimes the police come to know about are reported by victims, or those who represent them (eg, store detectives). The BCS asks about personal or household victimisation, so not surprisingly 94% of reported offences uncovered had been reported to them either by victims, or on their behalf by family or friends. The police were at the scene of the crime in only 3% of cases; assaults were most likely to be witnessed by the police themselves. Very similar patterns have been found in earlier sweeps of the BCS and in other research (eg, Burrows, 1982).

The police were most likely to hear of a crime by being phoned by someone involved; seven out of ten incidents came to their attention in this way. Overall, few callers resorted to the 999 service (12%), though this was used more frequently for a burglary (33%) or robbery (20%). The police were stopped in the street most often when a robbery or theft from the person was involved.

The police response

Respondents in the 1988 BCS who had reported offences were asked whether the police came to the scene where the incident happened (a question new to the survey). Visits to the scene will mean a house call for those reporting household offences and many incidents involving vehicles (over half of which took place around the home). For victims of personal offences, most encounters will take place away from home. The survey shows that in 65% of all personal offences the police came to the scene, while 61% of household offences resulted in a visit by an officer at home (see Table A.7, Appendix A). These figures will understate the number of victims who meet the police at some stage; some victims, for instance, go to the station themselves. Nonetheless, as they stand, the figures are high. They are expectedly so for burglary (91%) and assaults (75%), though even reports of vandalism (67%) and personal thefts (61%) usually resulted in a visit. (This indicates, incidentally, that when damage and theft incidents do get reported they will tend to be relatively serious.) These results denote a fairly active approach on the part of the police to making personal contact themselves with victims, or those closely involved.

However, another question shows that many victims did not get a great deal of feedback from the police about their case: 63% said they were not kept well informed of the progress of the police investigations or that the police had not investigated – though not all of them said they felt the need for more information. Those who felt they were kept least well-informed were victims of vandalism, burglary, thefts from motor vehicles, bicycle theft, and personal property thefts.

Respondents were also asked how well, overall, they thought the police had handled the matter they had reported. Just over a fifth (22%) said they were 'very satisfied', and 60% were 'very' or 'fairly satisfied'. Those who felt they had been kept well informed by the police, not surprisingly, rated police perfomance more highly (47% were very satisfied, as against 9% of those not well-informed). So did those for whom the police had attended the scene (24% as against 18% of others).

However, Table 5 shows that victims were markedly less satisfied with police performance in 1988 than they were in 1984. Apart from those reporting robbery/theft from the person (where the numbers are small and therefore subject to wide sampling error), there is a consistent drop in satisfaction across all types of victimisation. (Figures are given for those 'very satisfied', but there is a similar picture for 'very' and 'fairly satisfied' responses.)

Table 5
Satisfaction with police response 1984 and 1988, by offence

	'very satisfied' with the way police handled the matter		
	1984 %	*1988* %	*Change*
Vandalism	34	20	–14
Theft from motor vehicle	22	16	– 6
Burglary	30	23	– 7
Theft of motor vehicle	48	30	–18
Bike theft	33	21	–12
Other household theft	35	25	–10
All household offices	32	21	–11
Assault	37	23	–14
Robbery/theft from the person	19	30	+11
Other personal theft	24	21	– 3
All personal offences	29	23	– 6
All offences	31	22	–10

Notes:
1. Change between 1984 and 1988 is given as percentage points.
2. For this comparison, 1984 figures were adjusted such that incidents which the police care to know about other than through someone reporting them are excluded. If they are not, the satisfaction figures for 1984 are slightly higher.
3. Weighted data. Source: 1984 BCS and 1988 BCS (core sample).

Table A.8 in Appendix A shows changes in satisfaction with police response by area, age, sex, tenure and socio-economic status. Only victims in rural areas showed more satisfaction with police response since 1984 (although satisfaction was rather low to start with). By age, the most pronounced downward shift in attitudes was among those over 30, and particularly those over 50. The pattern of satisfaction increasing with age is still maintained in 1988, but the range is narrower. (This mirrors, incidentally, changes in satisfaction with the police generally). There was relatively little difference in shifts in attitudes between men and women – though men were slightly more dissatisfied in 1988. Satisfaction has fallen more among 'blue collar' (manual) workers.

Reasons *why* respondents said they were dissatisfied show that lack of effort and information seem most at issue (see Table A.9, Appendix A). It was much more common in 1988 than in 1984 to cite as a reason that the police 'didn't do enough' and/or that they 'failed to keep respondent informed of progress of the investigation'. Four out of ten of those dissatisfied also complained of lack of interest on the part of the police – a high figure, but similar to 1984. There is no evidence that the police were seen as more impolite.

Some new questions in the 1988 survey indicate the extent to which victims were offered help and information by the police. Of those who reported crimes, 1% said they had been offered help by the police additional to that given in the course of their investigations. A further 3% said they had asked for help. Of the two groups, a fifth said the police had given useful help or advice (a figure which could be depressed because some offers of help were not taken up). The vast majority of those who had not been given any help by the police or other outside agencies did not feel they wanted help. Of those who did, just over a third said help from the police would have been useful.

Among reporters, 3% were given information by the police about Victim Support Schemes. However, most referrals are made automatically to schemes without the victim being told, and in some areas the availability of voluntary resources may limit the degree to which the police can make referrals.[2] Bearing in mind that compensation through the courts or the Criminal Injuries Compensation Board may be relevant for only a proportion of victims, some 8% of victims of assault and 12% of victims where the police found out who did it were given information by the police about claiming compensation – in line with results of other research (eg, Newburn, 1988).

Ethnic minority reporting to the police

Tbe 1988 BCS included a 'booster' sample of Afro-Caribbeans and Asians to examine their attitudes and experiences compared with white respondents. Chapter 5 gives details of the sample and looks at their victimisation risks. At issue here is the experience of Asians and Afro-Caribbeans with regard to reporting crimes to the police.

For BCS offences as a whole, there was little difference in the level at which whites, Afro-Caribbeans and Asians reported to the police – perhaps contrary to what might be thought. Looking at individual offence categories, the only statistically significant difference was that both Afro-Caribbeans and Asians reported more burglary and vandalism to the home. This, though, seems largely explained by higher levels of loss and damage – a point taken up in Chapter 5 when the nature of victimisation among ethnic minorities is considered.

Satisfaction with the police after reporting, however, was lower among ethnic minorities, a finding anticipated in a survey in London in 1981 (Smith and Gray, 1985). In the 1988 BCS, 61% of white victims said they were, 'fairly' or 'very' satisfied with the way the police had dealt with the matter, as against 49% of Afro-Caribbeans and 44%

---

[2] Over 300,000 referrals were made to VSSs in 1987/8, virtually all from the police (NAVSS, 1988). Among 1988 BCS victims who had reported, 2.7% had asked for or been offered help by a VSS. Of these, 72% were burglary victims. Among those not given any help by the police or other outside agencies but who expressed the need for some help, a fifth mentioned VSSs.

of Asian victims. Both Afro-Carribbean and Asian victims were more likely than whites to feel that the police did not do enough. Afro-Caribbean victims more often perceived impoliteness or unpleasantness on the part of the police, and they were more likely to feel that the police should have apprehended the offender. Asian victims were relatively more dissatisfied because the police did not appear to be interested.

Summary

* Where victims had not notified the police of the offence against them, this was mainly because in their eyes the offence involved was trivial and not amenable to police action. Previous BCS analysis, however, has shown many incidents at the trivial end of the range are reported, and many regarded as serious by their victims are not.

* The crime workload of the police is heavily determined by the reporting behaviour of the public since the police are rarely in a position to discover crimes for themselves. The vast majority of crimes examined in the survey that the police come to know about were reported to them by victims or their close associates. Seven out of ten incidents were reported by phone, though the police came to the scene in two-thirds of incidents.

* The feeling that the police could not or would not want to deal with the offence is a minority reason for not reporting, though more people than in 1984 now appear not to report because of this.

* Of those who reported a crime, 22% were 'very' satisfied and 60% were 'very' or 'fairly' satisfied with the police response. However, the figures were higher in 1984. Those dissatisfied most often cited lack of effort, interest and information.

* Taking seriousness into account, there is little evidence that Afro-Caribbeans and Asians report crimes less often to the police than whites. However, they tend to be less satisfied with how the police deal with them when they do report.

4 Crime at work

So far, no special attention has been paid in the BCS to victimisation at work but the 1988 survey included some new questions about this[1]. The results have to be evaluated in the context of a limited amount of other research. Some 'occupation specific' studies have focused on workers apparently at risk of robbery (eg, Building Society staff (Austin, 1988), and Post Office workers (Ekblom, 1988)) or violence (Health Service workers (HSAC, 1987; Smith, 1987) – though their actual risks relative to other workers have not been measured. The early US National Commercial Crime Survey compared risks between businesses and households – but only burglary and robbery were considered and the focus was business not worker-based (US Dept of Justice, 1976; Skogan, 1978). Other research, using data from crime surveys, has focused simply on workers' experience of crime in general, rather than on offences arising out of the type of work they do.

Nonetheless some markers from previous research provide a context for BCS results. First, it has been shown that those in paid employment face higher risks than those not (ie, housewives, the sick, the retired), but lower ones than among the unemployed and those still in education. The factors which play a part are essentially those which 'lifestyle' or 'routine activity' theories have highlighted (see Garofalo (1987) for a summary). 'Non-workers' (leaving aside the unemployed) have a more domestic lifestyle which shields them from out-of-home offences, and they are also among the least demographically vulnerable (eg, being older, more residentially stable, etc). Workers have a more active, less homebound lifestyle which places them at greater risk, and they are disproportionately represented among younger people and men, who are more exposed to crime. The unemployed and students are younger still, and even more similar in other ways to offenders themselves, with whom they are more likely to be in contact. 1988 BCS data confirms this pattern (see Table A.10, Appendix A and Gottfredson (1984) and Widom and Maxfield (1984) for similar results from the 1982 BCS). Taking all personal offences, for instance, the unemployed have risks five times higher than the least victimised group (non-workers). Workers' risks are nearly three times higher than among non-workers. (Those working part-time are less at risk than full-time workers.) The pattern is evident for both sexes, though less marked among women. Whether or not they work outside the home, women may be more domestically constrained in ways which reduce their exposure to crime.

Second, background factors also seem to explain how risks, whether or not they arise at

[1] The questions were sponsored by the Health and Safety Executive Committee on Violence who wanted information about verbal abuse against workers, and the vulnerability of different workers to crime because of their job.

work, vary for workers in particular jobs. Most at risk are those in urban jobs, with a lot of young, male workers, a high turnover, low status, and irregular hours. In the United States, Block *et al.* (1984) found that, amongst others, restaurant staff and street sellers were particularly prone to assault, threats and robbery.

Third, while demographic factors strongly drive overall risk patterns, they have been found less useful in explaining offences specifically related to the jobs that people do. The studies here are limited in number, but they emphasise how risks at work might cut across demographic factors and be more explicable in terms of the tasks and responsibilities that different workers have. Analysis of large crime surveys undertaken in the United States (notably, Lynch, 1987; Collins and Cox, 1987) have been able to show that, in general, risks increase in jobs where workers:

* have tempting 'tools of the trade';
* handle money;
* have frequent contact with the public (especially a nuisance-prone public);
* have a mobile existence (going to and from the main worksite frequently);
* work in an environment felt to be unsafe; or
* are involved in a job which involves transporting goods or passengers.

It has also been found that some victimisations at work tend to be reported most often by better-educated respondents, which may indicate a response bias – a point discussed below.

In presenting results from the 1988 BCS results, the extent of verbal abuse by the public against workers is discussed first. (Such abuse was measured only in a brief set of 'screener' questions; full details were not collected in a Victim Form, and they are not counted as 'conventional' BCS offences.) The importance of work as the location of crime is examined second and, third, offences which victims thought were specifically related to their job.

Verbal abuse at work

Many workers regularly suffer verbal abuse from public. (Tired shoppers do not spare the feelings of shop assistants, for example, and those dealing with drunks may well get a torrent of abuse.) Tests of survey methodology suggest that asking people to recall, over a relatively long period of time, regular and usually unmomentous incidents like verbal abuse will produce an undercount: many incidents will simply be forgotten. Nor did the BCS tap whether workers themselves might have been at fault (for instance, by offering bad-tempered service or throwing in a few insults of their own).

Bearing in mind that the figures may well be underestimates, some 14% of those in work at the time of the interview said they had been verbally abused in the course of work by someone other than a colleague over the past 14 months or so (see Table 6).

Two-fifths of these said that they had been verbally abused just once or twice; a fifth said they had been in excess of 10 times. Men and women seemed equally prone. Younger workers (16-30), particularly younger women, were most likely to have been abused, or were perhaps more sensitive to it. There was no evidence that Afro-Caribbeans were more abused than whites, though Asians were very slightly more so.

Table 6
Percentage of workers who experienced verbal abuse by the public, by age and sex

	% who experienced one or more incident of verbal abuse			
	Men	*Women*	*Total*	*Unweighted N*
Aged 16-30	16.8	18.7	17.7	1711
Aged 31-45	17.0	13.0	15.2	2105
Aged 46 or more	8.5	9.0	8.7	1885
Total	14.1	13.6	13.9	5701

Notes:
1. Based on those in work at time of the interview. Incidents experienced over the recall period (1 Jan 1987 to interview, average 14 mmths).
2. Weighted data. Source: 1988 BCS (core sample).

Workers had been most frequently abused by an adult (this happened in over 60% of incidents). The adult was usually abusive on his/her own (the sex of the abuser was not asked). Youngsters seem to rely more on safety in numbers; nearly as many incidents involved a group (8%) as one youngster (10%). Drunks accounted for nearly one in ten of the incidents. In 80% of incidents workers were sworn at. Insulting comments about job performance were made in nearly 40% of incidents (often with swearing). In incidents against non-whites, over 60% involved some racial insult.

Adults were most likely to be foul-mouthed and critical about job performance. They picked on men and younger women, rather avoiding the elderly. Youngsters hurled their abuse (most often just swearing) more often at women and the elderly. One assumes that young offenders were mainly male, and no doubt they were reluctant to take on their own sex.

Work as the scene of crime

Given the average working day, employees are at risk at the worksite for long hours – longer than in the pub in the evening, though this will be a riskier place. A full 71% of incidents where workers' personal property was stolen happened in or around the workplace, and 56% for all BCS offences of this type (see Table A.11, Appendix A). Just over a fifth of assaults against workers took place at work, and nearly a third of threats. Figures for other offences were lower, but even so one in ten robberies and thefts from the person were at the worksite, and a slightly higher proportion than this of vehicle vandalism and thefts.

Crime due to workers' jobs

The workplace, then, is a frequent scene of crime. 'Exposure' is one of the reasons for this, and co-workers will be implicated in some offences. Of more interest is the extent to which victimisation is due to the nature of the work being undertaken (called hereafter 'job-related' crime)[2]. Analysis is mainly restricted – to maintain numbers – to three offences categories: (i) 'violence', comprising assaults and robbery; (ii) 'threats'; and (iii) 'thefts', both non-contact offences and the smaller number of thefts from the person, in which there was some offender-victim contact, but no violence or threat. Compared to other offences, these were by far the most job-related in nature.[3]

Workers blamed their jobs for nearly a quarter of violent incidents they experienced, more than a third of the threats, and more than a quarter of personal thefts (see Table 7). The public rather than fellow employees were blamed for nearly all threats, and three-quarters of violent incidents. However, only about half of the job-related thefts were blamed on the public. Many workers will have thought fellow employees were culpable (or could not be sure they were not), and for some workers their possessions will be in areas to which the public has no access.

Table 7
Crime among workers: offences due and not due to nature of the job

	not because of nature of job	*job–related*	*% of job-related incidents due to the public*
	%	%	%
Violence	77	23	74
Threats	64	36	92
Thefts	73	27	52

Notes:
1. Based on those in work at time of incident. Percentages based on rates of victimisation over full recall period.
2. Weighted data. Source: 1988 BCS (core sample)

Women and work

How do women fare when they work outside the home? Victimisation theory would posit that they should face more similar risks to working men than is the case among women and men in general – because they will have more coincident lifestyles and be more similar demographically (cf. Widom and Maxfield, 1984). The results largely bear this out (see Table 8). Though the risk of threats is higher among males generally and male workers, men as a whole face 1.8 times more *violence* than women; among

[2] The question asked of respondents in work at the time of the incidents was: 'Did the incident happen because of the nature of your job?'. Those who said yes, were then asked: 'Did it happen through coming in contact with someone in the course of your work, for example clients or members of the public, but *not* colleagues?'

[3] Not surprisingly, few people attributed household incidents to the nature of their work. Moreover, while a not insignificant amount of vehicle crime occurs at the workplace, relatively few offences were thought by workers to be because of the type of work they did (no doubt because they appreciated that cars are vulnerable wherever they are parked for long).

workers the sex difference is less, 1.6. Men generally are only slightly more at risk of *theft* than women – a narrower difference because women are particularly vulnerable to handbag thefts. Among working women, the risk of personal thefts is *greater* than among men: the slight advantage that women as a whole have disappears for women with more diverse, less domestic routines.

Table 8
Differential risks of crime among men and women

	Violence	*Threats*	*Thefts*
Total sample			
Differential risk, male:female	1.8	1.4	1.1
Current workers			
Differential risk, male:female	1.6	1.4	0.9
Job-related offences (current workers)			
Differential risk, male:female	1.4	0.9	1.6

Notes:
1. Current workers, those in work at time of the interview. Based on incidents experienced over the full recall period.
2. Core sample. Weighted data. Source: 1988 BCS.

However, for *job-related thefts* (in the third row of figures in Table 8), male workers' risks increase again: men are much more likely than women to experience thefts which are seen as due to the nature of their work – possibly because they often work in less office-bound environments, or have more 'tools of the trade' which are targets for theft. For *job-related violence and threats,* the picture is different. The overall advantage that women have as far as violence is concerned, eroded somewhat when they work, eroded further for offences blamed on the job – offences which both men and women said were usually due to the public rather than colleagues. For job-related threats, which again mainly involve the public rather than colleagues, women are *more* vulnerable than men. Half the threats which women workers reported in the survey were job-related, as against less than a third among men. As will be seen, this narrowing of risk is mainly due to higher-than-average reports of violence and threats at work among women in some particular occupations.

Occupation and risk

In sample surveys, the number of respondents in the groups featured in other research (eg, Building Society staff) will be too small to make comparisons. What can be done in the BCS is to look at the occupational groupings used in the Condensed Key Occupations for Statistical Purposes (OPCS, 1980). The jobs of workers are put into 161 catagories in this classification system, the categories aggregating to 17 occupational 'orders'. Table 9 shows which occupational categories faced high risks, and the 'order' in which they fell. Because of small numbers and error on the estimates of risks, a fairly stringent criterion of vulnerability is taken: a single asterisk denotes that risks were at least twice the overall average; double asterisks denote that risks were more than three times the average. In one case (the literary/artistic/sports 'order'), risks for the occupational 'order' are shown, because numbers in individual job categories is small. (Table A.12 in Appendix A shows the occupational categories which make up the headings shown in Table 9.)

Table 9
Occupations with above average job-related risks

	Violence	*Threats*	*Thefts*	*Unweighted* N
EDUCATION/WELFARE/HEALTH				
1 Higher education (men)			★	63
2 Teachers		★★	★	172
3 Welfare workers	★★	★★		71
4 Medical + dental practitioners			★★	22
5 Nurses (women)	★★	★★		143
LITERARY/ARTISTIC/SPORTS				
6 All the category			★	83
MANAGERIAL (1)				
7 Production + site managers (men)	★			80
8 Office managers (women)	★★			25
9 Retail + wholesale managers (men) (2)	★	★	★	113
10 Entertainment managers	★★	★★	★★	49
11 Security (men)	★★	★★		67
SELLING				
12 Sales reps (men)			★	96
PERSONAL SERVICES				
13 Waitresses and bar staff (women)			★★	35
14 Housekeeping + related (women)			★★	24

Notes:
1 Some non-mangerial workers are included in security.
2 Female retail and wholesale managers were also at risk of theft.
3 'Violence' comprises wounding, common assault and robbery; 'thefts' contact and non-contact thefts.
4 ★ = at least twice average overall risk. ★★ = at least three times average risk. Based on incidence rates over full recall period among current workers in same job as when victimised.
5 Categories with less than 20 workers in the sample are excluded.
6 Weighted data. Source: 1988 BCS (core sample).

Three technical points should be made. First, where risks for men and women differ, this could be because of sample size (there were very few male nurses in the BCS sample for instance). Second, some job categories include a variety of workers: 'housekeeping and related', for instance, comprises several different occupations broken down below the level of the 161 job categories coded (eg, travel stewards, ward orderlies, hospital and hotel porters); there is not way of knowing which particular jobs are riskiest. Third, some workers may be at high risk (eg, ambulancemen of violence), but they are not shown in Table 9 as numbers in the sample are very small.

One of the most vulnerable occupational groups is Education/Heath/Welfare (EHW). In this group, welfare workers (both male and female) were especially vulnerable to violence and threats. Teachers were prone to being threatened (and to verbal abuse, not shown in Table 9), but no teacher in the sample reported an incident of violence. Female nurses reported high levels of violence and threats, though the small number of male nurses did not.[4]

Thefts at work were relatively common among teachers, and among doctors and dentists. (In the EHW group, 30% of both men and women were teachers; 38% of the women were nurses; doctors and dentists formed 4% of the group).

Many of those in managerial positions also appear vulnerable across the range of offences. Production and site managers (nearly all of whom were men) were vulnerable to violence. Those managing either wholesale or retail business (eg, garages or shops) were also vulnerable, and to threats and thefts also. Violence was high among female office managers (not among men), though it is not possible to pinpoint the specific areas in which they worked, and numbers are small. Among those who managed pubs or other places of entertainment, risks of all the offences considered were high. Male security workers (there were few women) were particularly prone to violence, threats (and verbal abuse).

Thefts at work were relatively common among the 'literary/artistic/sports' category, particularly among men; photographers were at particularly high risk, as were 'entertainers' – though numbers are small. Job-related thefts were also higher than average among a category of salesmen which included 'reps', street sellers and scrap dealers. Within the category of 'personal service' workers, waitresses and female bar staff were prone to theft (there were few waiters and male bar staff), as were those in 'housekeeping and related jobs', which as said covers a variety of occupations. Not shown in Table 9 because of small numbers, were high risks of violence for male ambulance workers and hospital orderlies, and for a miscellaneous category of personal service workers which includes lift and car park attendants and 'bookies'.

It is not possible to say how far response bias affects these results. For instance, it might be argued that some occupational groups (eg, nurses) are particularly sensitive to assaultive behaviour because they feel themselves inadequately appreciated and remunerated. In addition, many of those who reported high risks of job-related offences were 'white-collar' workers. Some 'education effect' then could also be at work, either because while-collar workers are better at handling the task of the interview, and/or because they apply a different threshold as to what constitutes an

---

[4] Smith's (1987) study of workers in a large general hospital, half of then nurses, showed them to be at relatively high risk of threats, though not – compared to previous BCS data – to violence. Hospital workers were particularly vulnerable to thefts, both of and from cars and bikes (not included in the present analysis), and thefts of personal property. Not too much can be made of these differences, because of methodological factors: eg, the focus here is on offences which were seen to be because of job being done, rather than, as in Smith's study, on offences 'at work', whoever perpetrated them.

assault or threat against them for instance (see Gottfredson, 1986).[5] However, even if there is some response bias affecting the results, this seems unlikely to account fully for the patterns of risk – which are not inconsistent with other research. For instance, security personnel would usually be thought to be at high risk, and this is borne out by the results. Health workers face the out-of-sorts, those in welfare the unstable, and those in education difficult teenagers (cf. Dodge and Lentzner, 1984). Those who manage discos, off-licences, or take-aways have contact with clienteles who are younger and likely to be drinking. Those in the literary/artistic /sports category may have attractive things to steal, and doctors and dentists may be vulnerable to theft of drugs. Those working in pubs and restaurants may find it difficult to keep on eye on their personal property.

The two US studies of Lynch (1987) and Collins *et al.* (1987) suggested that job-activity variables were more powerful in explaining risks at work than demographic factors. In neither study was gender important after job-activity was taken into account: women workers were as vulnerable as men if their jobs involved 'high-risk' activities.[6] The present analysis suggests that its failure to find a gender effect on crime at work could possibly have been due to risks for women being affected by high levels of crime among particular occupational groups in which women are the main employees – eg, nurses and welfare workers.[7] In many ways, the picture of higher male victimisation when these occupations are set aside is more plausible. Men will usually work in riskier jobs (eg, security, nightclubs), and for longer and less regular hours (cooking the dinner constrains women's opportunities for overtime).

Moreover, higher male victimisation is often seen as linked to more assertive male behaviour patterns.

Characteristics of job-related offences

In terms of their objective consequences, job-related offences were not greatly different from other offences experienced by workers. Average losses for job-related theft were a little higher, but the difference was not large. Victims of violent incidents needed medical attention from a doctor in about the same proportion of job-related incidents

---

[5] In addition, blue-collar workers may have found difficulty with the notion that their job puts them in a particular situation at a particular time, and thus, perhaps, at risk of crime. This bias might have less effect on the reporting of job-related thefts, which were at similar levels among both white and blue collar workers. In any event, the similarity of risks is less remarkable: the protection afforded by the work environments of white collar staff may be offset by their fuller wallets and leather briefcases being attractive for theft.

[6] Lynch's (1987) study examined factors affecting victimisation at work using data from a special one-off supplement in the US National Crime Survey which measured work-related victimisation and 'work activity' variables. Collins and Cox's (1987) study used data from telephone interviews with workers in Washington, DC; unlike Lynch, they distinguished between violent offences (in which threats were included) and property offences (of theft and damage) The US measures were of victimisation *in the course of work,* rather than – as here – offences due to *the nature of the work being done.*

[7] The importance of these groups is clear. For instance, if the EHW category is omitted from analysis, risks of job-related violence changes from being 1.4 times higher for men than women to a full 2.7 times higher. The figures for threats are as revealing: whereas men are less at risk of job-related threats with EHW category in (0.9 times), the risk changes to 3.9 when it is omitted.

as other ones (about 15%). Some 6% of the job-related incidents considered resulted in the victim having to take time off work, as against 9% of other incidents. Workers (or their employers) notified the police in about four out of ten job-related incidents as against a third of others, though organisational requirements to report may play a part in this.

Previous research has already shown that the nature of crime committed against women is rather different from that against men, not only in the sense that women experience different types of crime (eg, more handbag thefts and fewer assaults), but also in their being exposed to a rather different type of offender (cf. Worrall and Pease, 1986; Widom and Maxfield, 1984; Mawby, 1988). Table 10 shows some differences in the characteristics of offences against men and women, both those which were job-related and those not. Mainly violence and threats offences are considered as the victim is most likely to be able to say something about the offender.

Table 10
Characteristics of job-related offences

	NOT JOB-RELATED		*JOB-RELATED*	
	Men	*Women*	*Men*	*Women*
	%	%	%	%
Female offender only*	4	13	4	18
One offender*	51	72	51	78
All/some offenders known to victim*	43	63	52	74
Offender school age				
Violence + threats	1	4	6	12
Thefts	9	14	5	22
Offender older than 25*	35	49	44	60
Offender drunk				
Violence	66	61	83	16
One day or more off work*	9	20	3	5
Needed to see a doctor				
Violence	11	25	20	3
Police knew about matter*	28	54	55	23

Notes
1 Based on those in work at time of incident. Offences are thefts, violence and threats unless specified.
2 The first six items are based on cases where the victim could say something about the offender.
3 Items asterisked based on threats and violence only.
4 Weighted data. Source: 1988 BCS, core sample.

For violence and threats *not* related to their jobs, women are more vulnerable than men to offenders who act alone, are better known to them, and either younger or older than 16-25. Rather more women offenders are involved, and the incidents concerned are rather more serious in that more medical attention is needed, more time is lost from work, and more offences are reported to the police.

For *job-related* offences, some of these patterns are repeated – and accentuated. Women still appear more vulnerable to being assaulted or threatened by another women (nearly a fifth of incidents involved a woman offender), a single offender, someone they knew, or someone of school-age, or older than 25. However, women are much *less* likely to encounter a drunk in job-related incidents than in incidents outside work, whereas a full 83% of job-related incidents of violence agains *men* involved a drunk. Moreover, the incidents of violence reported in the survey by women which happened because of their job seemed to have a less serious outcome. For instance, only 3% of women saw a doctor in job-related incidents, as against 20% of men. In parallel with this, fewer women notified the police after violence or threats than was the case with other offences, or with similar job-related incidents involving men.

Summary

* Those who go out to work are more at risk of crime than those not in the labour force, though risks are highest among the unemployed. The differences in risks among 'working women' and other women are rather less than among male workers and non-workers – perhaps because women's lifestyle varies less whatever they do.

* Work is the scene of much crime, though the time people spend there will largely explain this. Seven out of ten thefts of workers' personal property took place at work, though workers were not always sure who was responsible – colleagues or the public.

* Some 14% of workers said they had been verbally abused by the public over a period of rather more than a year. Being abused becomes less frequent with age. Men and women seem equally prone.

* Adults are most abusive. Youngsters who verbally abuse workers seem to need the company of peers more than adults, and they tend to avoid picking on men. Drunks are involved in one in ten incidents. In 80% of incidents workers were sworn at. Among non-whites, 60% of incidents involved racial abuse.

* Workers said that a quarter of violent offences and over a third of the threats they experienced were due to the work they did. A full half of threats against women were job-related, but having property stolen because of their job was commoner for men.

* Welfare workers and nurses reported comparatively high levels of violence and threats due to their job. So too did security personnel, and those who managed places of entertainment (pubs etc). Teachers were not vulnerable to violence, though they were to threats, verbal abuse and thefts.

* Offences which happened to male workers because of their job seemed a little more serious than other offences, though offenders were more often known. The

offenders involved were older than those who caused trouble in other contexts. In 83% of violent incidents the offenders were drunk.

* Offences which happened to women workers more often involved female very young offenders, and those who were sober. Women workers reported in the survey rather less serious incidents in the work domain, though outside it the offences women experienced were rather more serious than they were for men.

5 Ethnic minority risks

A new feature of the 1988 BCS was coverage of a 'booster' sample of Afro-Caribbeans and Asians to consider (i) whether they are disproportionately victims of crime; (ii) the extent to which there is a racial element in the offences they experience; and (iii) their interactions with the police. This chapter presents preliminary results on the first two issues. The third – interactions with the police – will be covered in a separate report (Skogan, forthcoming). Appendix C gives details of how the booster sample was chosen.

The number of Afro-Caribbeans and Asians picked up in the nationally representative core sample is small. Adding them to those interviewed in the 'booster' sample gives a bigger sample, though still small for highly refined analyses. Specifically, the two non-white groups interviewed were:[1]

i. Just over 700 'blacks', mainly West Indians but including a number of Africans. (The group is called Afro-Caribbean hereafter);

ii. Nearly 1,000 Asians: those from India, Pakistan and Bangladesh, particularly India.

It is important to note when looking at the vulnerability of ethnic minority groups (or any others) that the BCS deals only with selected crimes and threats. Questions are *not* asked about the array of incidents which can be hurtful but are not technically criminal: eg, nuisance behaviour, malicious complaints and refusal of service in shops etc. Also, although special effort was made to recruit ethnic minority interviewers and allocate them to areas with high minority concentrations, interviewers were not specifically ethnically matched to respondents in the booster sample – a point returned to.

Risks of crime

Overall, both Afro-Caribbeans and Asians are more likely to become victims of crime than whites, although this takes no account of the fact that their social and residential circumstances may play a part here. Table 11 shows the percentage of each group who

---

[1] Sampling was not meant to identify 'blacks' from different groups. In the Labour Force Survey, Afro-Caribbeans comprised 84% West Indian and 16% African (Shaw, 1988). This percentage is likely to be similar in the BCS. The 'Asian' group in the BCS is made up of Indians (61%), Pakistanis (32%) and Bangladeshis (7%). These proportions are very similar to those in the LFS. According to LFS figures for 1985-87, the Afro-Caribbean groups comprise about 1.2% of the population of Britain, and Asians about 2.3%. Together, the groups comprise about three-quarters of the non-white population.

were a victim once or more of different offences – so-called 'prevalence' rates[2].

Afro-Caribbeans are more likely to experience burglary (especially where there is a successful entry into their homes). Those who own cars and bikes are more prone to thefts than whites, and many of these thefts take place near home. Afro-Caribbeans are also more likely to be assaulted, threatened and to suffer robbery or theft from the person. However, they appear *less* at risk than whites of household vandalism.

Table 11
Differential risks of victimisation, by ethnic group

	Percentage victimised			
	White	*Afro-Caribbean*	*White*	*Asian*
1. Household vandalism	4.7	3.6–*	4.7	7.5**
2. Burglary	5.6	10.3**	5.6	6.2
Attempts + no-loss	3.2	4.7(*)	3.2	3.7
With loss	2.7	6.4**	2.7	3.5
3. Vehicle crime (owners)				
Vandalism	9.4	8.7	9.4	13.7**
All thefts	17.9	26.3**	17.9	19.5**
4. Bicycle theft (owners)	4.2	8.4*	4.2	3.9
5. Other household theft	7.9	6.9	7.9	9.3(*)
All household (1-5)	29.8	32.7(*)	29.8	35.5**
6. Assault	3.4	7.4**	3.4	4.4
7. Threats	2.5	3.9	2.5	5.3**
Assaults/threats	5.5	9.4**	5.5	10.8**
8. Robbery/theft from person	1.1	3.3**	1.1	3.0**
9. Other personal thefts	4.0	5.5	4.0	3.1
All personal (6-9)	9.6	16.1**	9.6	14.8**
Unweighted N	9874	733	9874	996

Notes:

1. Based on incidents occurring over full recall period.
2. All vehicle thefts includes theft of and from vehicles and attempts. Other household thefts include thefts in a dwelling. Risks of sexual offences are not shown because of small numbers. They are included in personal offences.
3. Double starred differences are statistically significant at the 5% level (two-tailed test, taking complex standard error into account). This means that the chances are less than one in twenty that the difference has arisen simply through sampling error. Single-starred differences are significant at the 10% level.
4. Figures in sub-categories (eg, attempted plus no-loss burglary and burglaries with loss) do not add to the total category (eg, burglary) as some people will have been victims of both kinds of offence.
5. Weighted data. Source 1988 BCS core and booster samples.

[2] Prevalence rates are not sensitive to the extent to which victims may be susceptible to repeated victimisation and the factors that determine this may be somewhat different from those that affect an individual's risk of becoming a victim at all (which is what prevalence rates measure). However, taking account of differences in the number of incidents experienced by whites, Afro-Caribbeans and Asians did not significantly alter the pattern of results.

Asians, in contrast, appear particularly vulnerable to vandalism compared with whites and those with cars were again more at risk of vehicle crime. For personal offences, Asians were more at risk of threats than whites and, like Afro-Caribbeans, at higher risk of robbery/theft from the person. Burglary and assaults were commoner among Asians although this could be due to sampling error: these risks were not statistically significantly higher for Asians. Thefts of personal property appeared less common among Asians, though sampling error could explain this.

The indications are, then, that for many crimes both Afro-Caribbeans and Asians are more disadvantaged. Both groups seem generally more vulnerable to property theft in and around the home, with Afro-Caribbeans particularly prone to burglary, and Asians to vandalism. Only Afro-Caribbeans are markedly more vulnerable to assaults, and only Asians to threats, but both groups face comparatively high risks of experiencing robbery and thefts from the person. Thefts of personal property (with no offender-victim contact) are no higher among the two ethnic minority groups than among whites.

There is little previous research with which to compare these results. It has usually been based on samples in particular localities, of slightly different ethnic origin, with the main focus on racial harassment (see FitzGerald and Ellis, 1989 for a review). Brown's (1984) national survey of West Indians, however, showed them to be more vulnerable than whites to assault, burglary and vandalism[3].

Relatively little in previous work speaks directly to the question of whether the vulnerability of ethnic minority groups is rooted in demographic factors which are known to be related to higher victimisation risks (eg, Gottfredson, 1984). But demographic differences between whites, Afro-Caribbeans and Asians in the BCS are often striking. The profiles, of course, are based on people who agreed to be interviewed, but they are generally close to the demographic picture drawn by the Labour Force Survey. The exception is an over-representation of Asian men in the BCS (60% of Asian respondents were men), which may reflect a reluctance among Asian women to take part, perhaps because of language and cultural factors.

In some respects, Afro-Caribbeans and Asians are more similar to each other than they are to whites (see Table 12). They are both, for instance, more likely to live in higher-risk ACORN areas (see Appendix G for details of the ACORN neighbourhood classification). They are both younger populations with higher rates of unemployment and lower household income. In other respects, Asians fall mid-way between Afro-Caribbeans and whites, though the characteristics of the areas that

---

[3] West Indians were found to be more at risk of theft from the person in London generally (Smith and Gray, 1985) and in Islington (Jones *et al.*, 1986). Crime statistics for the Metropolitan police district (Home Office 1989) showed that those of 'non-white appearance' were disproportionately likely to be victims of assault, robbery and other violent theft. In the inner city area of Manchester there were few differences between risks among whites and West Indians (Tuck and Southgate, 1981). In Coventry, Asians were found to be more at risk than whites of certain types of vandalism and burglary (Dawson *et al.*, 1987).

Afro-Caribbeans and Asians live in are likely to be different. Asian families, for example, are more likely than whites, but less likely than Afro-Caribbeans, to be headed by a younger person; and they tend to have lived in their area for longer than Afro-Caribbeans but for less time than whites. They see their immediate environment as less prone to crime than Afro-Caribbeans do, though not as salubrious as do whites. This is consistent with the number in each group who live in the highest-risk inner cities: 40% of Asians, a full 70% of Afro-Caribbeans, but only 17% of whites.

In some ways, though, Asians are a distinctive group. Many more were married than whites or Afro-Caribbeans; having children at home was much more common; and very few families had a female head (6%), unlike the third among Afro-Caribbeans. These factors may reflect in more home-bound routines, and fewer Asians, for instance, went out frequently at night. Owner-occupation among Asians was even higher than among whites and few (14%) were publicly housed – unlike Afro-Caribbeans, 45% of whom lived in council property.

Table 12
Demographic composition of different ethnic groups

	White	*Afro-Caribbean*	*Asian*
Male	48	47	60
Age 16-30	25	46	44
Married	64	43	72
Unemployed	12	25	24
Spent 2+ evenings out in week	44	43	31
Household characteristics			
Household head under 30	13	37	21
Female Household head	24	37	9
Children under 16	31	49	72
Single mother with dependent children	5	21	5
HH income over £10,000	35	27	25
Non-manual Household head	48	38	37
Owner-occupier	66	38	76
Area of residence			
Inner city	17	70	40
High risk Acorn area	39	80	70
'Good' condition housing	66	30	36
Lived in area 10+ years	64	34	42
Definitely won't move	50	29	39
Less crime than elsewhere	55	41	47
People help each other	40	33	56
Unweighted N	9874	733	996

Notes:
1. 'Unemployed' includes those unemployed at all during the previous year.
2. High risk Acorn areas include Acorn groups D, E, F, G, H, I.
3. Weighted data. Source: 1988 BCS core and booster samples. Afro-Caribbeans and Asians from the former are added to those from the latter.

The overall picture is one of Afro-Caribbeans being at the worst environmental disadvantage, living predominantly in inner cities, more transient and less residentially stable than Asians. They were typically younger than whites, as were Asians, though more often either single or heading one-parent families. Asians lived in more uniformly urban areas than whites, though less often than Afro-Caribbeans in inner cities. They were in tighter family structures, and seemed more socially tied to these.

Differential risk

Multivariate analysis was conducted to assess the specific importance of race in victimisation, taking account of demographic variables associated with higher risk. A series of LOGIT models were constructed separately for Asians and whites, and Afro-Caribbeans and whites, looking at offences which they were likely to experience significantly more often than whites (see Appendix B for details)[4]. Ethnicity as a factor in crime was considered for:

Asians:	Threats Vandalism Robbery/theft from the person (hereafter contact theft)
Afro-Caribbeans:	Burglary Assaults Contact thefts

Once demographic and other variables are taken into account, the picture of ethnic minority vulnerability changes. The greater likelihood of Asians becoming victims of *threats* was largely explained by differences between them and whites in terms of area of residence, sex, social class, age and marital status. Asians were not statistically significantly more likely to be threatened than with whites in similar demographic circumstances. Factors to do with area of residence and other demographics, however, did *not* explain higher risks of *vandalism* among Asians: ethnicity was an important factor. This was also true in relation to *contact thefts* against Asians. (Tables B.1, B.2 and B.3 in Appendix B gives results for threats, vandalism and contact thefts respectively.)

In contrast, differential risks between Afro-Caribbeans and whites were more likely to be accounted for by differences other than ethnicity. After accounting for age, family composition and aspects to do with where they lived, the greater *burglary* risk among Afro-Caribbeans disappeared (a finding consistent with Tuck and Southgate's 1981 study). Personal characteristics (age, sex and marital status in particular) largely accounted for differences in *assault* rates between whites and Afro-Caribbeans. The same factors (as well as inner city residence and tenure) were important in explaining risks of *contact thefts*. (Tables B.4, B.5 and B.6 in Appendix B gives results for burglary, assault and contact thefts respectively.)

---

[4] The variables included in each model were not always the same. They were chosen (on the basis of other analysis) for their relevance in explaining each kind of victimisation considered. However, existing knowledge of what is important in explaining victimisation is based on overall risk patterns and therefore mostly based on whites. Factors which affect victimisation among minorities may be slightly different, and further work could examine this.

Differences between areas were consistently important in explaining risks among both Afro-Caribbeans and Asians: living in the inner city, in an area with high social disorder and low 'stability' – measured for instance by the condition of dwellings, length of time in the area, and moving intentions (see Table B.1, Appendix B for details of the scale used). However, comparing Asians and whites, there is evidence that Asians are victimised rather more with regard to vandalism and contact thefts, irrespective of demographic factors.

Although the pattern of victimisation of ethnic minorities changes when factors other than race are taken into account, it is still noticeable that there is a consistent (albeit not always statistically significant) tendency for the ethnic minority groups to be victimised rather more for the offences considered. Moreover, the nature and circumstances of crimes they experience may still be different. In particular, as discussed later, ethnic minorities attribute racial motivation to many of the crimes they experience. It also seems that they may, when they are victimised, experience rather more *serious* offences than whites, and that the offenders involved differ somewhat.

Seriousness of the offence

For offences involving property theft and damage, both Asians and, in particular, Afro-Caribbeans were slightly more likely than whites to suffer higher monetary losses – in line with results found nationally by Brown (1984), and in Coventry (Dawson *et al.*, 1987). This was the case both in the inner city – where victims' losses tend to be generally higher – and elsewhere. The pattern is generally consistent across different offences. The need for medical attention following an assault or robbery (few victims needed to see a doctor except for these offences) was rather less for Afro-Caribbeans than whites, though the figures indicate that Asian victims were slightly more seriously hurt.

The offenders

Asian victims are more vulnerable to victimisation by groups of strangers: 27% of their incidents involved four or more offenders (19% for whites and 11% for Afro-Caribbeans). Also offenders were much less likely to be known, or if they were, only by sight. This supports the picture drawn in Coventry of Asian victims being much more subject to random attacks/harassment by passing groups of strangers (Dawson *et al.*, 1987). Afro-Caribbean victims reported more similar experiences to whites: over half the incidents against both groups involved a single offender, though Afro-Caribbeans were slightly more likely to know the offender well. Drunks were more often involved in incidents against white victims (30%) than in those involving Afro-Caribbeans (23%) or Asians (18%). Women were rather more involved as offenders when Afro-Caribbeans were victimised. The fact that Afro-Caribbean women are also rather more likely to be victims than whites and Asians would suggest a higher number of woman-against-woman incidents amongst Afro-Caribbeans. Being confronted by offenders with weapons in assaults, robberies and threats was a rather commoner experience for Afro-Caribbeans and Asians than it was for whites.

The vast majority of white victims (87%) reported that white offender(s) had been involved – sometimes with other racial groups. Afro-Caribbeans were much more likely than whites to have been victimised by other Afro-Caribbeans (38% were compared with 8% of white victims). Asians were more likely than whites to say that Afro-Caribbeans were responsible (they were in 19% of incidents against Asians). It was unusual for Asian offenders to be mentioned except in the case of Asian victims where 12% reported an Asian offender. The pattern of these results may reflect the fact that ethnic minority victims are more likely to encounter an offender from a minority group because of a higher concentration of ethnic minorities in the areas where they live.

The characteristics of incidents in which the three groups were involved are summarised in Table 13.

Table 13
Characteristics of offences experienced

	White	*Afro-Caribbean*	*Asian*
	%	%	%
Female offender only	8	17	6
Single offender only	51	58	33
Four or more offenders	19	11	27
All/some offenders known to victim	49	52	30
Offender known well	52	59	39
Offender (some or all)			
White	87	55	70
'Black'	8	38	19
Asian	2	—	12
Offender drunk	30	23	18
Needed to see a doctor			
Assaults and robbery	15	10	21
Losses of £25 or more			
Property crime	44	67	59
Offender(s) had weapon			
Assaults, robbery, threats	19	24	30

Notes
1. Based on cases where the victim could say something about the offender.
2. Weighted data. Source: 1988 BCS, core and boost samples.

The element of racial motivation

Afro-Caribbean and Asian respondents were asked whether they thought the offences they reported in the interview were racially motivated. In general, Asians were more likely to see them as so – some 24% of offences were said to be, as against 15% among

Afro-Caribbeans (see Table 14). Asians were also more likely than Afro-Caribbeans to leave open the possibility of racial motivation. An additional 14% of incidents prompted a 'don't know' answer; for household property crimes (in which it will often be difficult to be certain about motive) the figure was higher.

The offences for which Asians and Afro-Caribbeans most often felt there had been a racial element were assaults (44% for Asians, a third for Afro-Caribbeans), and threats (about half the incidents experienced by both groups). Asians more often said incidents of vandalism were racially motivated: a third were said to be, and in a further quarter of incidents there was some suspicion. More burglaries were also thought by Asians to be definitely or possibly racial. Asian women were particularly likely to see the threats and assaults they experienced as racial, though the number of incidents involved was small. Older Asians, too, tended more often to think that there was a racial element in these incidents. There is some indication that contact thefts were more often seen as racially motivated by younger Asians than by younger Afro-Caribbeans – though numbers are small for reliable comparisons. In contrast, it was Afro-Caribbean men rather than women who pointed to more racial assaults, though again Afro-Caribbean women, as did Asian women, saw more of the threatening situations in which they had been involved as caused by their race.

Table 14
Percent of incidents seen as racially motivated

	Afro-Caribbean		*Asian*		*Unweighted N*	
					Afro-Car.	*Asian*
	Yes %	DK %	Yes %	DK %		
Vandalism	20	1	32	23	29	94
Theft from motor vehicles	3	11	1	17	84	115
Burglary	1	6	9	23	78	79
Theft of motor vehicle	—	6	5	27	28	26
Other Household theft	1	3	4	6	70	95
Assault/sex	34	5	36	6	72	42
Robb/theft pers	5	1	14	2	30	37
Personal theft	—	2	3	8	38	33
Threats	44	5	50	15	39	47
Total	15	4	24	141	468	568

Notes:
1. Based on incidents over the full recall period.
2. Weighted data. Source: 1988 BCS core and booster samples.
Afro-Caribbeans and Asians from the former are added to those from the latter.

Where an incident was thought to have a racial element, victims were asked why they said this. The use of racist language was the main reason given by both Afro-Caribbeans and Asians, particularly the former. Asians were rather more likely than Afro-Caribbeans to see an incident as racially motivated because they felt it was something only comitted against their minority group, or that it had happened to them before, involving the same people.

Racial disadvantage?

The picture drawn is of Afro-Caribbeans and Asians tending to be more vulnerable to a range of crimes than whites. This is an important finding in its own right even though, in large part, it is explained by their over-representation in groups more prone to crime – for instance, council tenants, younger households and those in areas where disorder and crime are commoner. When account is taken of this, the particular vulnerability of Afro-Caribbeans and Asians is lessened – though not removed entirely. There is a consistent tendency for them to be victimised more than whites, though the statistically most robust 'race effect' is for Asians in relation to vandalism and contact thefts.

Whether response bias is affecting these results in a way as to understate the disadvantage of ethnic minorities is unclear. As said, interviewers and respondents were not ethnically matched – a costly procedure and with rather uncertain results (eg, Johnson and Cross, 1984). It is generally felt that differences in responses between matched and unmatched interviews are most likely in relation to attitudinal and sensitive questions, rather than those about actual experience. Other definitional and threshold response effects may be linked in too, though on balance the data suggests that the ethnic minority respondents reported offences across the range of seriousness[5]. There is no way of knowing whether the question about the racial element in victimisation was considered sensitive by booster sample respondents, or indeed whether in the context this would have led them to underplay racial factors. In any event, Afro-Caribbeans and Asians certainly reported many offences against them which they saw as having a racial basis. Being threatened because of race is very common; both Afro-Caribbeans and Asians were also often racially assaulted. For Asians, evidence or suspicion of a racial element in property offences is relatively frequent.

The extent to which racially motivated crime adds to overall risks among ethnic minorities needs to be addressed separately for Afro-Caribbeans and Asians. For Afro-Caribbeans, their risks are higher chiefly because of demographic and residential factors. Racially motivated crime could add to these risks to a degree (and be particularly upsetting), but is it difficult to think that Afro-Caribbeans would be *less* at risk than similarly-placed whites if racially motivated offences were not counted. Response bias cannot be entirely ruled out in deflating 'other' victimisations; or it may be in some incidents a racial element is an unfortunate, additional causal factor.

Asians seem more disadvantaged by their ethnicity. Their overall risks are generally higher than among whites – in part because of other factors, though less so than Afro-Caribbeans whose social and family circumstances are less favourable. Race itself

---

[5] Afro-Caribbeans reported rather fewer property offences with low values, but locality will play a part here. The pattern of results regarding the need for medical attention, too, does not suggest that minor assaultive incidents are being omitted, though these have been found to be the most likely incidents to be susceptible to response 'productivity' (Skogan, 1986).

appears to contribute directly to higher risks for some crimes among Asians, and this is more often perceived by them to be the case. For contact thefts, it may be that – unlike Afro-Caribbeans – Asians are seen by offenders as passive or 'easy' targets. Their greater vulnerability to vandalism reflects the fact that they live in rather more disorderly and less cohesive localities than whites (as is the case for Afro-Caribbeans), but additionally their ethnicity seems used against them.

The extent to which ethnicity is *directly* implicated in increasing the risk of victimisation, then, is a difficult issue. Nonetheless an underlying racial disadvantage for ethnic minorities is evident in that they are more vulnerable to crime, even if only because their circumstances put them in more unstable and crime-prone areas. The fact that their collective experience is different from that of whites will have consequences both for their perceptions about crime, and their quality of life.

Summary

* Both Afro-Caribbeans and Asians tend to be more at risk than whites for many types of crime. This is largely explained by social and demographic factors, particularly the areas in which they live. However, taking account of this, ethnic minority risks still tend to be higher, with Asians particularly at greater risk of vandalism and robbery/theft from the person.

* Afro-Caribbeans and particularly Asians see many offences against them as being racially motivated. Being threatened and assaulted because of race is common. For Asians, evidence or suspicion of a racial element in property offences is relatively frequent.

* For offences involving property theft and damage, both Asians and Afro-Caribbeans were slightly more likely than whites to suffer higher monetary losses.

* Asian victims are more vulnerable to victimisation by groups of strangers and to rather more serious victimisations. Afro-Caribbeans were more likely know 'their' offender well. Afro-Caribbeans were more likely than Asians, and much more likely than whites, to be victimised by other Afro-Caribbeans.

6 Neighbourhood Watch

Neighbourhood Watch has made more of an impact, in terms of its visibility if nothing else, than any other community crime prevention effort in Britain. In 1984, just over half of the BCS sample had heard of Neighbourhood Watch and by 1988 the figure was 90%. Potential support is widespread with two-thirds of those currently not members expressing willingness to join a scheme if one were set up in their area. Actual schemes have proliferated and the time and resources invested in launching and implementing them has increased accordingly. From BCS estimates, 14% of households were members of schemes at the beginning of 1988, some two and a half million households in England and Wales. The figure may well now be higher.

In other parts of Europe and North America Neighbourhood Watch (or Block Watch) is also enjoying popularity. Programmes may cover as many as 25% of the Canadian population (Nuttall, 1988), while even in 1984, 19% of households in the USA reported a NW programme existed in their area, with 7% participating (Whitaker, 1986). Schemes are also underway in many Western European countries.

Neighbourhood Watch can be seen as a formal extension of some activities which already take place informally in many residential areas – in particular keeping an eye on neighbours' property, watching out for suspicious behaviour, and reporting untoward events to the police. Neighbourhood Watch 'packages' these activities with some other measures. Its main idea is that residents will deter potential offenders by increased surveillance, and more frequent reporting to the police. Increased reporting is also intended to improve the chance of an arrest, thus taking offenders off the streets. Apart from the possibility of reducing crime, Neighbourhood Watch is felt to play a valuable part in alleviating fear and increasing community cohesion as residents in an area come to know and rely on each other. A local co-ordinator is appointed and newsletters and/or leaflets may be distributed to keep members up-to-date on activities or to give general crime prevention advice. Members are encouraged to be more security conscious by, for instance, marking property and having a security survey. The fact that residents belong to a scheme is often signalled by street signs and stickers in the windows of members' homes. The general intention is that such schemes should be *community based*, though *supported* by local police, with the extent of formal police involvement varying from scheme to scheme.

We know relatively little about the characteristics of members, the activities they actually engage in, and the effectiveness of schemes in reducing crime and fear. In this country, Husain (1988) surveyed a sample of schemes from their co-ordinators' point of view. The 1984 BCS provided some information on *potential* support for NW at a national level before it became widely known (Hough and Mayhew, 1985; Hope, 1988). In terms of whether NW has been effective in reducing crime and fear, the number of careful evaluations is limited, and results are mixed. Most evaluative work has been done in North America, and much of it has been criticised on methodological grounds. Rosenbaum (1988) cites two thorough evaluations. One in Seattle showed a reduction in crime, but a marginal increase in fear (see Lindsay and McGillis, 1986). The other was an even more sophisticated test of four schemes in Chicago (Rosenbaum *et al,* 1986); there was no consistent effect on crime or disorder, and in three areas fear increased. In this country, a study of a scheme in Kingsdown (Veater, 1987) provided some evidence of a fall in crime. Forrester *et al*, (1988) found a reduction in burglary on the Kirkholt estate in Rochdale after the setting up of a number of 'cocoon' NW schemes involving a small number of households. An evaluation by Bennett (1987) of two schemes in London – supposedly well-run though neither in the event particularly active – showed no evidence of crime reduction, but a decrease in fear in one of the schemes.

The 1988 BCS provides an opportunity to look at the characteristics of ordinary members and their schemes on a national level. The survey is not ideal for studying how NW changes people's perceptions of crime, or their risks – for which longitudinal data is needed. But given the topicality of NW and the relative scarcity of research evidence, it is useful to examine what the BCS *can* say about:

* who is best catered for by schemes?
* what do 'members' do?
* Is there evidence of success?

Scheme coverage and membership

There are some fairly marked regional differences in scheme coverage (see Table 13, Appendix A). The North West, South East, Northern and West Midlands regions have the most schemes, while the South West, Yorkshire and Humberside, East Midlands, East Anglia and Wales have markedly fewer. Regions with the best NW coverage appear to prompt higher levels of joining than regions where coverage is lower – ie, where there are fewer schemes, residents are also slightly less likely to join them. Schemes often evolve from spontaneous action on the part of the public, though support from the police is important in getting schemes off the ground and they themselves sometimes make the initial move (a quarter of schemes in Husain's (1988) study were initiated by the police). Differing attitudes among police forces as well as residents, then, have no doubt influenced how NW has developed within regions. But active commitment on someone's part produces both more schemes and better public support when they are set up.

Table 15 gives details of scheme coverage and membership levels according to the ACORN classification of neighbourhoods (see Appendix G for details of ACORN). Schemes were most common in 'affluent suburban areas', 'high-status non-family areas' and in areas of 'modern family housing with higher incomes'. Membership levels were generally high here too, though they were also high in some other areas where scheme coverage was slightly lower (eg, 'better-off retirement areas'). Those in multi-racial areas and the poorest council estates, where only 13% said there was a scheme in their area, were least likely to join (57% joined if there was a scheme). The other council estates out of the poorest category also had low scheme coverage, but rather higher joining levels.

Areas where membership was lower also tended to be those where burglary risks were higher. This result is in line with Husain's (1988) survey of schemes, and with much North American research which shows that they emerge more among those with a strong commitment to community groups than those necessarily facing the biggest threat from crime (eg, Lewis and Salem, 1981). An exception to this pattern in the BCS was 'high status non-family areas' (ACORN group I); these are usually in inner cities and cover affluent households with few children in areas where there are large houses and flats in rental accommodation. Risks are high here and membership also relatively high. Overall though, schemes appear to be less common in areas of greatest need, *and* local residents are less likely to join even if a scheme has been set up.

Table 15
Membership of Neighbourhood Watch schemes, by ACORN neighbourhood group

	Scheme set up in respondent's area	*Take-up rate where schemes set up*	*Members of schemes as % of sample in each area*	*% of hhlds burgled in 1987*
	%	%	%	%
HIGH COVERAGE AREAS				
Affluent suburban areas	29	84	24	3
High-status non-family areas	25	70	17	11
Modern family housing, higher incomes	22	77	17	3
Better-off retirement areas	17	84	13	2
Older housing of intermediate status	17	79	13	3
Agricultural areas	17	78	12	2
LOW COVERAGE AREAS				
Poorest council estates	13	57	7	13
Better-off council estates	11	78	8	5
Multi-racial areas	12	57	7	6
Poor quality older terraced housing	10	76	8	6
Less well-off council estates	10	73	7	7
NATIONAL AVERAGE	18	78	14	5

Notes:
1. The '% of households burgled' includes attempted burglaries.
2. Weighted data. Source: 1988 BCS, core sample.

THE 1988 BRITISH CRIME SURVEY

The 1988 BCS results suggest that the 'typical' NW household[1] is one which:

* owns or is buying the house/flat;
* has a head of household aged over 30 years;
* has an above average income; and
* lives in a low burglary risk area.

More detailed statistical analysis can pinpoint the importance of socio-demographic factors associated with joining a scheme (see Table B.7, Appendix B for details). Each of them is important independently of each other. Thus, although higher-than-average household income is associated with owner-occupation, for people with the same level of income, owner-occupiers are more likely to be members. Analysis also allows that the factors interact in different ways for different groups. Council and private renters are unlikely to become members even when they have a high income, but they are more likely than might be expected to become members if they live in high-risk areas.

What do members do?

NW is meant to promote both activities which are seen as of general use in deterring crime (eg, property marking) and those which are more specific to NW (eg, putting stickers in windows and attending meetings). In particular, though, it seeks to encourage people to watch out for suspicious behaviour and to report such incidents to the police.

Members of NW schemes use 'general' crime prevention measures more than non-members (see Table 14, Appendix A). For instance, 10% of members had a security survey by the police, compared to 4% of non-members;[2] a third had marked property (12% non-members), and two thirds had told their neighbours when their house was empty (58% non-members). But often they had done these things before joining NW: for example, about half of those who had a security survey or marked bicycles had done so before they became members. The indications are, then, that the greater security activity among NW members may partly reflect the fact that they join NW because of their general predisposition to take precautions.

To examine activities linked specifically to NW membership, respondents were asked a series of questions about what they themselves had done, and what the scheme had done for them. Table 16 gives the results. Three–quarters of members had put stickers or posters in their windows and knew the name or telephone number of their local co-ordinator; about a quarter had attended at least one meeting in addition to the initial meeting at

---

1. Households are counted as 'members' if they answered 'yes' to the question: 'Do you consider your household to be a member of the scheme?' Those who are typical scheme members are very similar to what the 1984 BCS showed to be the typical 'supporter' of NW at a time when schemes were much less common – ie, those who were most likely to say they would join (Hough and Mayhew, 1985).

2. These figures appear high compared to other research. Laycock (1989) found 1% of Surrey residents sought a survey in 1986, while in Bennett's (1987) study 4% of NW members in two London schemes had security surveys. However, these studies cover a shorter time period; BCS respondents were asked if they had ever had a survey while they had lived at their present address.

which the scheme had been set up. A proportion of members seemed rather inactive: 21% had neither attended progress meetings nor knew the name of their co-ordinator; 8% had done neither of these nor put up stickers or posters.

Moving from scheme members to the scheme as a whole, putting up street signs was most common: four out of five schemes had done this. In addition to street signs, another four-fifths of schemes had *either* produced a newsletter or leaflet, *or* given members information about the scheme. Only 4% of schemes could be classified as 'inactive' insofar as they had neither fixed NW signs, produced newsletters or leaflets, nor kept members informed about how the scheme was working.

What of the single most significant activity associated with NW: watching for and reporting suspicious behaviour? Respondents were asked if they had seen anything in their area that they thought might be a crime or which might lead to a crime being committed. Very slightly more NW members (18%) than non-members (16%) said that they had seen something. Though not a statistically significant difference, this may nonetheless denote that NM members are alert to suspicious incidents, given that one might suppose they are less common in the lower-risk areas best covered by NW schemes.

Table 16
Neighbourhood Watch activities

	% of members
INDICATIONS OF MEMBER ACTIVITY	
Put stickers or posters in window	77
Knows name or telephone no. of co-ordinator	73
Attended meeting other than first	27
INDICATIONS OF SCHEME ACTIVITY	
Signs put up in area	81
Receives newsletters occasionally or often	53
Received information from police or co-ordinator about how scheme is working	37
Receives crime prevention leaflets occasionally or often	36

Note:
1. Weighted data. Source: 1988 BCS, core sample.

Table 17 shows what people saw and what they did about it. NW members were much more likely to have interpreted what they had seen as being a burglary; non-members were more likely to think that someone was comitting vandalism. While it is difficult to say whether people were judging what was going on correctly, members could be especially sensitised to burglary. In terms of what action was taken, NW members more often reported the matter to the police. To discount the possibility that this reflected demographic characteristics independent of their membership, members and non-members were matched on age, tenure, income and area of residence. The higher level of reporting among members remained (45% reported as against 31% of non-members). Neither was this explained by the fact that members tended to witness potentially more serious incidents: of those who witnessed 'burglaries' 65% of members but only 42% of non-members reported these to the police. One cannot rule out that it might have been somewhat easier for members to report because of higher telephone ownership, but nonetheless the indications are that people in NW schemes *are* more likely to inform the police of suspicious incidents.

Table 17
Witnessing and reporting of incidents, members and non-members

	Member %	*Non-member* %
Witnessed possible crime	18	16
What did you think might be going on?		
Burglary	42	24
Vandalism/criminal damage	15	27
Car theft/theft from car	15	12
Assault/fighting	9	9
Shoplifting	1	3
Mugging	–	1
Other theft	2	2
Drug offences	1	3
Other	15	19
Don't know	–	1
Told police (matched sample)	45	31
Unweighted N		
Witnessed possible crime	726	4653
Type of incident	130	752

Notes:
1. Results on reporting to the police are only given here for the matched sample. Of all non-members, 29% had reported the incident to the police.
2. Weighted data. Source: 1988 BCS, core sample.

Is Neighbourhood Watch a success?

Whether or not NW is a 'success' can be judged in several ways. If the concept is popular and members perceive benefits, this is one criterion of effectiveness; a reduction in crime is a second, and a reduction in fear is a third. The BCS data has something to say on all three, though in terms of crime and fear it cannot provide definitive answers.

Popularity

The widespread popularity of NW schemes is demonstrated by the fact that membership has increased at a high rate since 1984 and that two-thirds of non-members are willing to join a scheme if one were set up. For existing schemes as was shown, most members and their schemes are reasonably active. Few schemes have fallen by the wayside: some 91% of schemes were said to be still functioning at the time of the survey, 2% had ceased and 7% of respondents were unsure if the scheme was still operating. The majority of current members felt that the level of interest in their scheme had stayed the same since it started, 22% felt that interest had gone up and only 11% thought that interest had gone down.

About half of members thought that there had been benefits from the scheme although 38% felt unable to judge. When asked if the scheme had reduced crime, 43% thought that the scheme had done so, althougth 41% – perhaps not surprisingly – felt unable to say. In his survey of NW co–ordinators, Husain (1988) found that a 'greater sense of security' was the most cited benefit *expected* from a scheme, followed by 'reduction in crime'. Improved relations with the police and improved community spirit were far behind these two in the list of expectations. The *actual* 'benefits' of schemes as perceived by members turn out to be similar (see Table 15, Appendix A) . If one interprets the response that 'people's homes are watched' as relating to an increased sense of security in some way, then this, followed by reduction in crime, are by far the most important benefits. Improved neighbourliness was mentioned by 13% of members, but only 11% specifically referred to reduced fear. Some 16% of respondents thought that one of the benefits was that they had become more alert to the risk of becoming a victim, a point returned to.

Reduction in crime

While it is useful to know that members feel that their schemes are of benefit, more important in policy terms is whether schemes reduce crime and fear of crime. As said, the BCS data cannot answer this question with any precision. The fullest information the survey provides relates to the experiences of householders at one point in time (so–called cross–sectional data). Assessing whether schemes reduce crime or fear of crime, is better done through specially designed longitudinal studies, which follow through the same or similar groups of people before and after they join schemes.

One question that the BCS can address is whether members faced lower chances of crime in 1987 than non–members. A first look shows that they did not: for instance, 5% of both members and non–members were victims of burglary or attempted burglary in 1987.[3] This is rather surprising as we know that members are better placed than non–members insofar as they live in lower–risk areas and are usually less vulnerable owner–occupiers. In any event, a stricter approach is to compare members and non–members, taking such risk factors into account. This was done by matching each NW household with a non–member household on income, tenure, age, and area of residence. The rate of burglary (including attempts) among matched non–members drops to 4%, as against 5% of members – a difference which is not statistically significant.

For evaluating the effectiveness of NW schemes, however, the better test is to see if members were better off *after* joining a scheme. The best measure in the current BCS is risks of *burglary with loss* among members and non–members in a five–year period, from the beginning of 1982 to the end of 1986.[4] For various reasons, this is an imperfect

3. These figures exclude those who joined schemes in 1987. This is the fairest test as there would have been little chance for NW to have had an effect. Also, it is difficult to tell from the data available when the burglaries against 1987 joiners occurred in the year – ie, before or after they joined. Burglary rates are focussed on here on the grounds that most emphasis within NW schemes is on burglary prevention.

4. As part of the offence screening process on the 1988 BCS, respondents were asked if anyone had got into their home and stolen things during the previous year (ie, it was a question about burglaries with loss). Whether or not the household was such a victim was decided on the basis of their answers to subsequent questions. The same screening question was put to respondents, asking about burglaries with loss since the beginning of 1982, in addition to any they had mentioned for 1987.

measure of 'pre-NW' burglary risks, but it allows some comparison of earlier risks with those in 1987 to see whether vulnerability to burglary changed in any way.[5]

The proportion of members and non-members who experienced a loss-burglary in 1987 was the same, at 3%,[6] but during the earlier period 1982-1986, NW members suffered a significantly higher risk (12% had a loss-burglary) than non-members (8%).[7] Members, then, show a larger drop in risks ($p < 0.05$), suggesting that joining NW made them less vulnerable than previously.

However, though encouraging, this finding cannot be taken as firm evidence of the effectiveness of NW in reducing burglary. Why members had a relatively high level of risk earlier on is difficult to explain. Some response bias cannot be ruled out, such that members - generally more sensitive to burglary – recalled more distant incidents better. Another more obvious possibility is that members joined schemes directly as a result of a burglary. This cannot be discounted for some members, though it is unlikely to explain things fully. If victims feel the need to take action after a burglary, they can certainly join a scheme *if* there is one, but most local residents have already joined in these circumstances, as has been shown. Victims could also start a scheme from scratch, but it is difficult to think that many have the time or energy to do this.[8] Perhaps the most plausible explanation is that residents or the police seek to introduce schemes in areas where crime is high - specifically to try and remedy the situation. Even though in general schemes are commoner in lower-risk areas, it may well be that within them schemes are started in the riskiest pockets. An unusual spate of burglaries may have prompted a scheme – and the high pre-1987 risks of members shown above would be reflected in this. Or pocketed risks could endure, which would help explain why in 1987 current member of NW were at no less risk of burglary than others. To repeat the point, though, further research is needed to test the effectiveness of NW on crime, preferably using panel or longitudinal techniques.

---

5. This analysis takes no account of *when* households became members of NW or when they were burgled during 1982-1986. Some households could have been members at the time they experienced their burglary, though this is relatively unlikely since NW is a fairly recent phenomenon: 83% of the group said their scheme had started in 1986 or 1987, rather than earlier.

6. It is not particularly appropriate to exclude pecple who had joined NW in 1987, as was done earlier (see footnote 3). At issue here is the relationship between risks among members and non-members over time. However, analysis excluding those who joined in 1987 produced substantially the same results.

7. These figures will underestimate the 'real' annual risks during the period since crimes occurring some way back are more likely to be forgotten than more recent incidents (cf. Skogan, 1986).

8. Evidence is mixed on the relationship between joining NW and victimisation. Bennett's (forthcoming) analysis did not observe any difference in joining among those previously burgled and not. From the 1988 BCS, being a victim of burglary was again not associated with being more *prepared to join* a scheme if one was set up – though behavioural intentions could change in the light of events. An exact two–thirds of burglary victims and non–victims were prepared to join (see Hope, 1988, for similar results from the 1984 BCS).

Reduction in fear

Implicit in NW is that fear of crime will be alleviated as residents come to have more of a sense of control over crime, both through their own efforts and those made on their behalf by neighbours. The BCS does not have sophisticated measures of this sense of control, and it is limited for investigating the full nuances of anxiety about crime – which has generally proved taxing for researchers.[9] Neither did the survey try to assess how anxious members were before joining NW, so it cannot address directly whether anxiety changed after joining: a specially designed longitudinal study could do this job better. But with these caveats, the BCS has something to say.

With regard to a sense of control, it appears that members do feel slightly better protected by the greater effort they have made with household security for instance. Amongst members, 53% thought that improved locks, etc made them a lot safer, as against 48% of non-members; and more members (56%) than others (50%) felt that an intruder would only get into their home with difficulty. This stronger belief in the efficacy of precautions, however, does not seem to follow through to being less worried about burglary: 60% of members said that they were very or fairly worried about being the victim of burglary, compared to 55% of non-members. Fuller analysis shows that this was not simply due to members being the type of people who are generally more fearful: membership of NW was independently associated with being worried about burglary taking account of other factors which previous research has shown to be related to fear: eg, sex, perceptions of risk and disorderliness, the crime level in the area, and previous victimisation (Maxfield, 1987; Box *et al.*, 1988). (Table B.8, Appendix B gives details of this multivariate analysis.) Other research has shown the same result; for instance, Bennett (forthcoming) showed that participants in schemes in Acton and Wimbledon were more fearful than those who did not join.

How does one interpret the fact that being a member of NW goes with being more worried about burglary? Having been burgled in the past is strongly associated with worry about burglary, both among scheme members and others. But even excluding those who had been burgled since 1982, members still appeared more worried. An alternative reason could be that those who are more fearful in the first place join schemes. In the 1988 survey, 61% of those who were very or fairly worried about being burgled said they would join a scheme if one existed, as against 47% of those who were more apathetic (cf. Hope, 1988, for similar results from the 1984 survey).

In addition, it might be that worry is inevitably reinforced by the means through which householders are encouraged to participate in NW: increasing their sensitivity to risk. The BCS data cannot testify to this conclusively, though it is not inconsistent with some other research. Certainly NW members here *are* more alert to the chances of crime. For

9. A number of measures of fear of crime were taken in the 1988 BCS. The most appropriate here is the question: 'How worried are you about having your home broken into and something stolen?' Those who said they were 'very' or 'fairly' worried are counted as 'worried' in the text.

one, they seem as ready to perceive suspicious behaviour in their generally salubrious neighbourhoods as non-members are in their less salubrious ones; they are also more likely to report suspicious incidents to the police. A not insignificant proportion of members (16%), too, cited as a 'benefit' of joining the fact that they 'had increased awareness of the risk of being burgled'. And among members generally, more (35%) thought they were likely to have a burglary in the next year than non-members (27%) – a pattent consistent across each ACORN neighbourhood group (see Table A.16, Appendix A). (In actual fact, between 4-5% will fall victim on 1987 figures, which shows as the 1984 survey did that householders substantially exaggerate risks.)

It is not hard to see why members could feel more worried after joining – as indeed in a sense they are meant to be. In attending meetings, they may be told about recent local burglaries and may even meet more victims than they would otherwise have done (previous research has shown that contact with or information about other victims increases fear (Maxfield, 1987; Skogan and Maxfield, 1981)). Having a home security survey may open up to members previously unnoticed ways in which a burglar could enter their home.

In sum, then, on the limited measures available, NW members appear to have a rather stronger sense that the precautions they are taking are helping them. This, though, does not result in their being less worried about burglary than non-members, even accounting for demographic differences which we know are associated with being fearful. The higher levels of worry among members almost certainly reflects the propensity of the more anxious to join NM in the first place. Their anxieties could be sustained by NW to the extent that it deliberately draws attention to risks as part of the process of suggesting ways of dealing with them. Whether worry about burglary as measured here signifies undesirable fear is a moot point. For some people it might; for others it might express only a more reasonable sense of apprehensiveness which could actually be valuable in encouraging more security consciousness. 'Fear of crime' is a complex issue and there is still much to be learned about whether increasing awareness of risks can be achieved without feeding undue anxiety.

Summary

* 14% of households were members of NW at the beginning of 1988, and two-thirds of those who were not were willing to join a scheme. Membership rates are highest in the North-West and South-East, and lowest in East Anglia and Wales. In areas where most schemes are set up, public support is stronger: more join schemes than they do when schemes are thin on the ground.

* Members tend to be better-off, owner-occupiers with a rather older head of family. They are most likely to live in 'affluent suburban areas'. Those on the poorer council estates and in racially mixed city areas are least likely to join NW. 'High status' inner city areas are the exception to the rule that schemes are most common in lower-risk areas.

* Members of NW are more security conscious (eg in having a security survey, or marking their property). However, their greater security awareness was a factor in their support of NW: many had taken precautions before joining.

* Three-quarters of members had put stickers in windows and knew their co-ordinator; a quarter had attended a meeting after the one set up to launch the scheme. Four out of five schemes put up street signs, and the same number had given out information about how the scheme was working. Few schemes were said to have collapsed.

* Members are much more likely than non-members to report suspicious incidents to the police.

* Members most appreciated a greater sense of security from having their home watched, and the feeling that NW deters crime. Many members, though, found it difficult to point to specific benefits of their schemes, or to say whether it had reduced crime.

* More detailed longitudinal studies are best for seeing whether NW reduces crime. The data available here are consistent with burglary risks being lower after joining NW though not definitive proof.

* NW has achieved its aim of making members more alert to the risks of crime. They are, though, more worried about burglary. This was no doubt a factor in their joining NW, and scheme activities may inevitably sustain this worry in trying to foster an awareness of risk.

7 Summary and discussion

This report has presented an overview of findings from the 1988 British Crime Survey, the third in a series whose main aim is to provide an estimate of the extent of crime which is independent of offences recorded by the police. Interviews were conducted with a representative 'core' sample of 10,392 people in England and Wales, and a 'booster' sample of 1,349 Afro-Caribbeans and Asians. They were asked about their experience of victimisation and about various other crime-related topics.

The 1988 survey confirms a number of results from the two earlier ones. For instance, it shows the predominance of offences against property in the BCS crime count (particularly those relating to motor vehicles), the shortfall between survey estimates of offences committed and the number recorded by the police, the extent to which different types of offences are reported to the police, and the main reasons why incidents go unreported. However, as the third in the series, the 1988 survey is able to say more about trends in crime over this decade. It also provides new information about crime at work (Chapter 4), risks of crime among ethnic minorities (Chapter 5), and Neighbourhood Watch schemes (Chapter 6). The main, new findings in this report are:

Trends in crime

* Crime in 1987 was higher than the last survey's figures for 1983, though the rate of increase (21%) was not quite as rapid as that of recorded crime (26%). Compared to 1981 figures from the first survey, the BCS increase in crime (30%) was lower than recorded crime (41%) - a statistically significant difference. This reflects a general increase in reporting to the police. Of BCS offences comparable with police statistics coverage, 41% were reported in 1987, as against 36% in 1981.

* The BCS indicates that the increase in different offences was generally higher between 1981-83 than it was between 1983-87 on an annual average basis.

* The most comprehensive BCS estimate of violent crime (wounding, robbery and common assault) shows a relatively modest increase of 8% since 1981.

* Offences which can be reliably said to have risen more in police figures than in the BCS are: vandalism, thefts from motor vehicles, and wounding/robbery.

* Bicycle theft has risen more according to BCS estimates than police figures. A fall in reporting may explain this in part, perhaps reflecting a drop in insurance cover as insurance companies have come to want separate cover for bikes. Changes in recording practices could also be implicated.

Burglary

* Burglary has also risen more according to BCS estimates, though due principally to an increase in attempted offences – which may indicate that better security is making entry harder for burglars. A drop in reporting may partly explain the divergence between BCS estimates and police statistics, and possibly some recording change.

* Looking at burglaries with loss over a considerably longer period, however, shows that recorded offences have substantially exaggerated the increase in burglary. The BCS and the General Household Survey combined indicate an increase in burglaries 1972 to 1987 in the region of 20%, as against about 125% in police statistics.

Reporting to the police

* When the police were not notified by victims this was mainly because they considered the offence involved not serious enough. The feeling that the police could not or would not want to deal with the offence is a minority reason for not reporting, though more people than in 1984 now appear not to report because of this.

* Of those who reported a crime, 22% were very satisfied and 60% were very or fairly satisfied with the police response. However, the figures were higher in 1984. Those dissatisfied most often cited lack of effort, interest and information.

Ethnic minorities and crime

* Both Afro-Caribbeans and Asians tend to be more at risk than whites for many types of crime. This is largely explained by social and demographic factors, particularly the areas in which they live. However, taking account of this, ethnic minority risks still tend to be higher. Asians are particularly at greater risk of vandalism and robbery/theft from the person.

* Afro-Caribbeans and particularly Asians see many offences against them as being racially motivated. Being threatened and assaulted because of race is common. For Asians, evidence or suspicion of a racial element in property offences is also relatively frequent.

* Asians are more vulnerable to victimisation by groups of strangers, and to rather more serious victimisations. Afro-Caribbeans were more likely know 'their' offender well. Afro-Caribbeans were more likely than Asians, and much more likely than whites, to be victimised by other Afro-Caribbeans.

Crime and work

* Work is the scene of much crime, though the time people spend there will largely explain this. Seven out of ten thefts of workers' personal property took place at work.

* Workers said that a quarter of violent offences and over a third of the threats they experienced were due to the work they did. A full half of threats against women were said to be job-related. In 83% of violent offences against male workers which were job related, the offenders were drunk.

* Welfare workers and nurses reported comparatively high levels of violence and threats due to their job. So too did security personnel, and those who managed places of entertainment (pubs etc). Teachers were not vulnerable to violence, though they were to threats, verbal abuse and thefts.

* Women reported rather less serious incidents which happened because of their work than men. For other offences, though, the reverse was the case.

Neighbourhood Watch

* 14% of households were members of NW at the beginning of 1988, and two-thirds of those who were not were willing to join a scheme. Membership rates are highest in the North-West and South-East, and lowest in East Anglia and Wales. In areas where most schemes are set up, public support is stronger: more join schemes than they do when schemes are thin on the ground.

* Members are much more likely than non-members to report suspicious incidents to the police. They are also more security conscious (eg, in having a security survey, or marking their property). However, their greater security awareness was a factor in their support of NW: many had taken precautions before joining.

* Three-quarters of members had put stickers in windows and knew their co-ordinator; a quarter had attended a meeting after the one set up to launch the scheme. Four out of five schemes put up street signs, and the same number had given out information about how the scheme was working. Few schemes were said to have collapsed.

* NW has achieved its aim of making members more alert to the risks of crime. They are, though, more worried about burglary. This was no doubt a factor in their joining NW, and scheme activities may inevitably sustain this worry in trying to foster an awareness of risk.

Discussion

Trends in crime

The BCS covers a six-year span over which survey-measured trends in crime can be compared to the picture from recorded offences. Though the trend pattern is not consistent across individual offence categories, for the broadest count of offences the 1988 survey shows a less steep increase in crime since 1981 than do police statistics. This reflects the fact that (for a variety of reasons no doubt) the number of offences the police are told about has increased, and for some offence categories at least, the number of these which are recorded is higher. The BCS only measures a selection of notifiable offences recorded by the police, and recorded crime figures will continue to be relied on, not least as an indicator of the workload of the police. Nonetheless, the survey demonstrates the scope for error when drawing conclusions about crime trends solely on the basis of statistics of recorded offences. It lends credibility, moreover, to explanations of rising crime which have tended to be neglected – that, for example, people's sensitivity to petty crime may have increased, leading to increased reporting to the police; or that additional police resources and greater efficiency in recording practice have led to increased recording of crime.

The sharpest example of the shortcomings of recorded crime figures as a 'barometer' of crime trends comes from the wide divergence over the period 1972-1987 between police figures and survey estimates for burglaries with loss, combining GHS and BCS data. Over the shorter timescale of the BCS, the divergence in the trend for wounding and robbery is particularly notable, since the wider category of 'violence against the person' recorded in *Criminal Statistics* has increased steadily over the decade, putting something of a 'dampener' on recent falls in certain property offences. The survey sets the picture only until the end of 1987, and only for burglaries with loss can it plot the trend over recent, individual years. Recorded offences suggest a peaking of burglary in 1986, and a downturn since then – a pattern similar for other property crime. Survey results are not inconsistent with this for burglaries with loss though the evidence is not conclusive. Nonetheless, the BCS suggests that the increase in many offences was steeper between 1981 and 1983 than after 1983 – again consistent with a slowing down of risks. Changes in the number of people most prone to law-breaking may play some part, though it is unlikely to be the full explanation: males in the early twenties have risen in number since 1981, though there were 7% fewer 14-20 year old males in 1987. The movement in crime levels in the near future will be of special interest to check whether the underlying upward trend is altering.

Crime prevention

One reason why the volume of property offences might fall is increasing security on the part of potential victims. A small pointer in this direction is that failed (ie, attempted) burglaries have risen more than successful burglaries recently. That there is an increase at all should not be ignored, but at least it may indicate that householders are making the burglar's job harder. The results reported in Chapter 6 on Neighbourhood Watch schemes seem to endorse a greater awareness among householders of their own responsibilities for thwarting law-breakers. Interest in schemes is high, members have been made alert to the risks of burglary, and they appear to be more likely to take action on seeing suspicious incidents. But while much attention is paid to burglary as an offence for which better security may pay dividends, the current results highlight other areas where better preventive measures are called for. For instance, thefts in and immediately around the work-site comprised over half of all thefts of personal property reported in the survey. It may be difficult to do much about many of these, but employers could at least give some thought to their security arrangements, and to offering workers better facilities for securing their possessions.

Thefts of and from vehicles comprise nearly a fifth of the crime uncovered in the BCS. Some owners may facilitate theft by carelessness, though more perhaps are vulnerable because of lack of garaging facilities (eg, those in inner cities), or convenient garage space (eg, council tenants). Many vehicle thefts take place in car parks, in shopping precincts and by railway stations for instance. Better management and supervision of these could help; considerable success has been achieved in New South Wales recently with new security measures in high-risk car parks (NRMA, 1989). The pool of cars on the road without newer, sophisticated security devices will remain large enough for some time to provide thieves with plenty of opportunities for stealing items from cars, or the cars themselves. Good security is however now becoming much more evident in vehicle design, and motor manufacturers should be reassured that two-thirds of 1988 BCS vehicle owners said they would be quite willing to pay more for a comprehensive security system if buying a new car.

Victims and the police

Skogan in his forthcoming report on the police component of the 1988 BCS will consider interactions between the police and the public across the full range of contacts they have with each other. The current results bear only on police performance with regard to those who report crime. Satisfactory service is likely to have wide benefits. Victims will talk to others about their experiences, and the police response will be part of the conversation. Moreover, victims who feel they have been well-handled seem less likely to fear future victimisation (Poister and McDavid, 1978; Parks, 1976).

Many victims had no complaint about how they were dealt with: 60% were very or fairly satisfied; 54% felt that they had enough information, or (if not) did not want more. But these are not large majorities, and they seem to be shrinking. Current policing policy has accepted the need for better provision for victims and in due course new initiatives should pay dividends. At the beginning of 1988, though, victims still wanted three things.

First, they wanted to be kept *better informed* – a request that has emerged in many other studies in this country and elsewhere (see Mayhew, 1985, for a review). Follow-up visits by regular officers are heavy on resources, and for many offences the police may have little information to pass on. Nevertheless, better and well-enforced standard procedures to relay *some* information might help, even if this only involves a standard letter format, or a brief telephone call.

Second, victims' perception of lack of police interest or commitment suggests the need for a more *involved and supportive response.* From the police perspective, many incidents will appear mundane and hopeless, but victims themselves will place more importance on what has happened. Research indicates that victims do not necessarily expect the offender to be 'bought to book', but rather want sympathy, reassurance, and due attention given to the 'rituals' of investigation as recognition that something untoward has occurred (cf. Newburn and Merry, forthcoming). Demeanour is one issue, which is low-cost but with obvious training implications. Another is doing more to help victims in terms of emotional support and practical advice – despite officers' claim that they have no time for 'victim work' (Newburn, 1989). Consideration has been given in this country to specialised victim 'after-care' units (offering a more accessible information point, speeding the return of stolen property and easing some practical problems), and Waller (1982) claims success for these in Canada. A cheaper and easier option, would be to build up closer links with outside agencies – and to make facilities for help better known. Relatively few 1988 BCS victims were offered information about claiming compensation through the courts or the Criminal Injuries Compensation Board (though admittedly it will not be relevant for many). Neither were many given information about Victims Support Schemes. Currently, some types of victim in some forces are automatically referred to VSSs schemes anyway, though even so recent research suggests that ordinary officers might negotiate formal procedures better, and tell victims about schemes more often (Maguire and Corbett, 1987; Newburn, 1989).

Third, the police may need to explain better why they have apparently not put more *effort* into following up a crime report. Information is one aspect of this. The way calls are attended to is another. It has been shown that direct contact between the police and victims was common in 1987 after a crime report was made, and this added to the victim's satisfaction with the police response. A quick response time may not necessarily be a priority as long as victims are told they will be dealt with, and when. Graded response initiatives, whereby the type and speed of action is determined by the nature of a call, use police resources well, but they may be problematic in public confidence terms unless the police can be flexible in dealing with victims of minor incidents who nonetheless seem upset. Similarly, 'case screening' methods, in which certain incidents are dropped after an initial investigation, are resource efficient but also potentially problematic from a victim viewpoint. 'Formal' screening allied to telling the victim why further action has been abandoned may be better than informal procedures which leave the victim in the dark. A fundamental problem is that public expectations are probably out of line with what the police can actually do about many reported incidents, and the public may need to be 'educated' about this. Doing it without undermining public confidence in reporting will need careful thought.

Risks of crime among ethnic minorities

A new issue considered by the 1988 BCS, and one not covered well by other studies, was whether ethnic minorities are more vulnerable to crime than whites. Asians in particular appear most disadvantaged: they face higher risks for some crimes than would be expected from their social and residential circumstances, they have a strong feeling that many crimes against them have a racial element, and the offences they experience are rather more serious. The present analysis is not exhaustive, and there is room for further work with the data, in particular to elucidate better the circumstances of ethnic minority victimisation. In any new research, the extent and nature of technically non-criminal racial harassment should be considered alongside criminal victimisation, and a check should be made as to whether the race of the interviewer affects the information respondents give.

Crime at work

Another new area of risk analysis was that of crime at work. Apart from the frequency of thefts at the workplace, as already mentioned, it showed that nearly a quarter of the violent incidents and a third of the threats uncovered by the survey were seen by workers as due to the type of work they do. This adds a new dimension to the picture of crime in which the predominant image has been of vulnerability on the streets. The analysis also raised pointers about how the nature of personal offences against women may vary from that against men, both at work and out of it. These bear further examination.

Taking stock

The BCS was mounted to offer an empirical base for assessing statistics of crimes recorded by the police, and to learn more about the nature of crime that private individuals face. The facility of the survey to pinpoint particular groups most at risk of crime promised to be of practical value in crime prevention programmes, while the procedure of having changing topic components offered the chance to acquire new information at national level about a range of issues (such as fear of crime), which could be more expensive to collect in specially mounted studies. On all fronts, the survey was meant to offer a boost to criminological research and theory, but above all to provide criminal justice policy-makers – and others – with a more comprehensive picture of the crime problem and the public's attitudes to it.

The 1988 BCS data will be deposited, as data from the other two surveys were, in the ESRC Data Archive to enable outsiders to make use of it. The scope for further analysis on the first and second surveys may by now be limited, though there is a great deal of material in the 1988 survey still to be examined. There will also be benefits from combining the three sets of data to look at particular issues (eg, the nature of robbery) for which numbers are small from one survey alone.

Loss of comparability with earlier surveys is an inevitable problem in changing the way the survey is conducted, but there is undoubtedly room, for instance, for improving measurement of some types of crimes (eg, sexual offences and domestic assault) for which some local surveys have produced apparently more complete counts with slightly different techniques. Another possibility for the future is to devote more space to particular offences (eg, street crime, vehicle theft, or multiple victimisation). Additional questions on the precise nature of what happened could be valuable, as well as better measurement of exposure to risk. The BCS has already made some theoretical contribution in attempting to relate crime risks to direct measures of lifestyle, but it is clear that lifestyle factors relate in different ways to different offences. More focussed measurement would enable a better understanding of why particular people fall prey to particular offences, and the circumstances in which this happens.

Appendix A
Supplementary tables

Table A.1
Rates of victimisation in England and Wales, 1981, 1983, and 1987: British Crime Survey estimates

	1981	1983	1987		*% change* 1983–87	*% change* 1981–87
		Rates per 10,000 HHs				
HOUSEHOLD OFFENCES						
1. Vandalism	1481	1504	1521	+/–127	1%	3%
2. Burglary	409	492	612	+/– 80	24%**	50%**
Attempts and no loss	205	248	345	+/– 57	39%**	68%**
With loss	204	244	267	+/– 55	9%	31%*
3. Theft in a dwelling	81	70	58	+/– 29	–17%	–28%
4. Theft from motor vehicle	702	827	1083	+/– 94	31%**	54%**
5. Theft of motor vehicle	156	153	200	+/– 34	31%**	28%*
6. Bicycle theft	118	155	201	+/– 42	30%	70%**
7. Other household thefts	845	918	946	+/–129	3%	12%
PERSONAL OFFENCES		*Rates per 10,000 people*				
8. Sexual offences	15	32	29	+/– 20	[–9%	93%]
9. Common assault	362	365	372	+/– 70	2%	3%
10. Wounding	131	108	141	+/– 50	31%	8%
11. Robbery	42	37	44	+/– 19	19%	5%
12. Theft from the person	112	129	79	+/– 20	[–39%	–29%]
13. Other personal thefts	410	442	447	+/– 68	1%	9%
ALL HOUSEHOLD OFFENCES	3791	4120	4610	+/–299	12%**	22%**
ALL PERSONAL OFFENCES	1065	1100	1099	+/–136	–0%	3%

Notes:
1. Starred figures are statistically significant at the 5% level (two-tailed test) taking complex sampling error into account. This means that the chances are less than one in twenty that the difference has arisen simply through sampling error.
2. Rates for 1987 are shown with the range in which they are likely to lie taking sampling error into account. Only women were asked about sexual offences; rates are per 10,000 females.
3. Categories 2, 7, 8, 9, 11, 12 and 13 include attempts.
4. Rates for 1981 and 1983 are, for some offence categories, marginally different from those previously published. Some recoding of offences was done to ensure consistency across the three surveys. Tighter classification of theft from the person in 1988 has reduced the figure here, while questionnaire changes account for the rise in sexual offences after 1981.
5. Weighted data. Source: 1982, 1984 and 1988 (core sample) BCS.

Table A.2
Levels of recorded and unrecorded crime, 1987: British Crime Survey estimates

	British Crime Survey			Criminal Statistics		
	Best Estimate (000s)	*Number reported* (000s)	*% reported*	*Offences recorded by police* (000s)	*% recorded of reported*	*% recorded of BCS best estimate*
1. Vandalism	2931	703	24	305	43%	10%
2. Burglary in a dwelling	1180	743	63	483	65%	41%
3. Theft in a dwelling	112	19	17	47	[247%]	42%
4. Theft from motor vehicle	2087	835	40	626	75%	30%
5. Theft of motor vehicle	385	366	95	333	91%	86%
6. Bicycle theft	387	240	62	133	55%	34%
7. Other household theft	1823	474	26	n.a.	n.a.	n.a.
8. Sexual offences	60	13	21	10	77%	17%
9. Common assault	1493	493	33	n.a.	n.a.	n.a.
10. Wounding	566	243	43	118	49%	21%
11. Robbery	177	78	44	30	38%	17%
12. Theft from person	317	108	34	39	36%	12%
13. Other personal theft	1794	556	31	n.a.	n.a.	n.a.
All BCS OFFENCES	13292	4918	37			

Notes:
1. Definitions of offences are in the Glossary.
2. The figures in first column are derived from applying BCS rates to the 1987 household population of England and Wales (for categories 1 to 7), and to the population aged over 15 (for categories 8 to 13). Only women were asked about sexual offences; the figures are based on women only.
3. Categories 2, 7, 8, 9, 11, 12 and 13 include attempts.
4. Offences recorded by the police are rounded to the nearest 1000.
5. Weighted data. Sources: 1988 BCS, core sample; *Criminal Statistics for England and Wales, 1987* with adjustments.

Table A.3
Rate of vehicle offences in England and Wales, 1981, 1983 and 1987: British Crime Survey estimates

	1981	*1983*	*1987*		*% change 83–87*	*81–87*
			Rate per 10,000 households			
1. Theft from vehicles	702	827	1083	+/–94	31 **	54 **
2. Theft of vehicles	156	153	200	+/–34	31 **	28 **
3. Attempted vehicle theft	98	158	222	+/–44	41 **	127 **
4. Vandalism to vehicle	850	919	841	+/–86	– 8	– 1
ALL THEFTS (1–3)	955	1138	1503	+/–115	32 **	57 **
ALL VEHICLE CRIME (1–4)	1806	2056	2344	+/–148	14 **	30 **
			Rate per 10,000 owners			
1. Theft from vehicles	1025	1372	1533	+/–120	12 *	50 **
2. Theft of vehicles	232	270	282	+/– 46	4	22
3. Attempted vehicle theft	142	230	313	+/– 58	36 **	120 **
4. Vandalism to vehicle	1256	1383	1191	+/–117	–14**	– 5
ALL THEFTS (1–3)	1398	1873	2126	+/–146	14 **	52 **
ALL VEHICLE CRIME (1–4)	2654	3256	3316	+/–193	2	25 **

Notes:
1. Double–starred differences are statistically significant at the 5% level; single starred at the 10% level (two–tailed test, taking complex standard error into account).
2. Rates for 1988 are shown with the range in which they lie taking sampling error into account.
3. The rates on the basis of owners refer to offences which were committed against owners themselves. There were a small number of cases in which non–owners had property taken from other people's vehicles.
4. 'Attempted vehicle thefts' cover attempted thefts of and attempted thefts from motor vehicles; it is often difficult to distinguish between the two. The very large increase since 1981 probably reflects, in part, non–sampling measurement error.
5. Weighted data. Source: 1982, 1984 and 1988 (core sample) BCS.

Table A.4
Annual average increases in crime, 1981–83 and 1981–87
British Crime Survey estimates

	Annual average change 1981–3	*Annual average change 1983–7*
HOUSEHOLD OFFENCES		
Vandalism	1.5%	1.4%
Burglary	10.4%	6.8%
Attempts and no loss	10.7%	9.8%
With loss	10.1%	3.4%
Theft from motor vehicle	9.3%	8.2%
Theft of motor vehicle	–0.4%	8.1%
Bicycle theft	15.3%	7.9%
Other household theft	5.0%	1.9%
PERSONAL OFFENCES		
Common assault	1.0%	1.1%
Wounding	–8.7%	7.6%
Robbery	–5.7%	5.1%
Other personal thefts	4.4%	0.9%
ALL HOUSEHOLD OFFENCES	5.0%	4.0%
ALL PERSONAL OFFENCES	2.1%	0.6%
ALL OFFENCES	3.9%	2.8%

Notes:
1. Theft in a dwelling is not shown separately because of small numbers. Sexual offences and theft from the person are also not shown because of coding inconsistencies. Totals of household and personal offences include these categories.
2. Weighted data. Source: 1982, 1984 and 1988 (core sample) BCS.

Table A.5
Percent of BCS estimated number of offences recorded by the police, 1981 and 1987

	1981	1987	1981	1987
	% recorded of reported		*% recorded of BCS best estimate*	
HOUSEHOLD OFFENCES				
1. Vandalism	33	43	7	10
2. Burglary	71	65	47	41
Attempts and no loss	41	37	20	16
With loss	88	85	74	73
3. Theft from motor vehicle	94	75	28	30
4. Bicycle theft	92	55	59	34
PERSONAL OFFENCES				
5. Wounding	41	49	17	21
6. Robbery	24	38	11	17
Wounding and robbery	37	46	15	20

Notes:
1. Definitions of offences are in the Glossary.
2. Weighted data. Sources: 1988 BCS, core sample; and *Criminal Statistics for England and Wales, 1981 and 1987,* with adjustments.

Table A.6
Reasons why the police were not notified, for selected offence categories

	Vand	*Tht frm MV*	*Bur*	*Bike tht*	*Tht dwl*	*Oth HH tht*	*Wng*	*Com ast*	*Rob*	*Tht frm per*	*Oth per tht*	*Ast*	*Tht p/ rob*	*All*
	%	%	%	%	%	%	%	%	%	%	%	%	%	%
Too trivial; no loss or damage	57	60	54	21	18	56	25	27	16	53	46	27	42	48
Police could do nothing	26	30	17	19	11	19	13	8	31	30	17	9	30	21
Police would not be interested	12	13	11	8	5	12	3	5	23	7	7	4	12	10
Fear/dislike of police	—	—	—	2	—	—	—	2	5	2	1	2	3	1
Inappropriate for police; dealt with matter ourselves	5	4	6	19	47	5	37	27	5	8	11	29	7	11
Reported to other authorities	4	2	4	1	7	4	—	7	—	2	19	5	2	6
Fear reprisals	2	<1	4	1	—	—	5	2	2	1	—	3	2	1
Inconvenient	<1	2	1	3	3	2	1	2	5	2	1	2	3	2
Other; vague	13	8	20	38	22	14	26	29	34	16	16	29	22	17
Unweighted N	538	748	215	89	40	572	69	206	26	72	295	275	98	2895

Notes:
1. Question: 'Did the police come to know about the matter? If not, why not?' (Multiple answers allowed.)
2. Incidents which occurred in 1988 are included. Thefts of motor vehicles and sexual offences are excluded because of small numbers, though they are included in 'All offences'.
3. Weighted data. Source: 1988 BCS (core sample).

Table A.7
Whether police came to scene, by type of crime

	% police came to scene
Vandalism	67
Theft from motor vehicle	42
Burglary	91
Theft of motor vehicle	51
Bike theft	35
Other household theft	63
All household offences	61
Sexual offences	60
Assault	75
Robbery/theft from person	41
Other personal theft	61
All personal offences	65
ALL OFFENCES	63

Note:
1. Weighted data. Source: 1988 BCS (core sample).

Table A.8
Satisfaction with police response 1988/1984, by selected variables

	% very satisfied				
	1984	*1988*	*change*	*1988 N*	*1984 N*
AGE					
16–30	20	18	– 2	761	723
31–50	33	23	–10	1022	983
51+	55	27	–28	215	174
SEX					
Male	30	20	–10	1004	990
Female	32	24	– 8	1004	909
AREA					
Inner city	30	21	– 9	660	722
Metropolitan	34	22	–12	468	391
Urban	34	19	–15	332	344
Mixed	35	25	–10	326	268
Rural	15	24	+ 9	222	174
TENURE					
Owner-occupier	33	25	– 8	1371	1089
Other	27	17	–10	635	655
SEG					
Non-manual	33	27	– 6	973	771
Manual	29	17	–12	981	926
RACE					
White	na	22	na	1880	na
Afro-Caribbean	na	14	na	183	na
Asian	na	11	na	251	na
OVERALL	31	22	– 9	2008	1755

Note:
1. Weighted data. Source: 1984 BCS and 1988 BCS (core sample).

Table A.9
Reasons for dissatisfaction – 1988 and 1984

	1984	1988
Didn't do enough	30	40
Weren't interested	38	39
Failed to keep respondent informed	21	34
Were impolite/unpleasant	3	5
Kept me waiting/slow to arrive	9	7
Made mistakes/handled matter badly	5	6
Didn't recover property	14	15
Didn't apprehend offenders	18	21
Unweighted N	467	588

Notes:
1. Percentages do not total 100% because multiple answers allowed. Not all response options shown.
2. Weighted data. Source: 1984 BCS and 1988 BCS (core sample).

Table A.10
Risks of crime among the unemployed and workers relative to non-workers

	Unemployed: Non-workers		*Workers: Non-workers*		*Unemployed: Non-workers*	*Workers: Non-workers*
	Men	*Women*	*Men*	*Women*	*All*	*All*
Personal thefts	6.8	6.6	5.3	4.2	6.2	4.5
Threats	6.5	1.9	3.7	1.3	3.3	1.9
Assaults	12.2	4.1	6.1	1.9	6.6	3.2
Robbery/theft from person	4.4	2.9	2.2	1.9	2.6	1.6
ALL PERSONAL OFFENCES	8.2	3.7	4.8	2.1	4.9	2.8

Notes:
1. Figures based on rates per 10,000 adults. Incidence rates over the full recall period are used.
2. Work status refers to the respondent's situation in the week prior to interview. Workers include full and part-timers; non-workers include the sick, retired, housewives and 'other'; the unemployed include students.
3. Weighted data. Source: 1988 BCS (core sample).

Table A.11
Incidents occurring at the workplace

	Inside work	*Out of doors at work*	*Work car park*	*Street near work*	*All work*
	%	%	%	%	%
THOSE IN WORK AT TIME					
Personal thefts	65	5	1	1	71
Threats	24	5	<1	1	31
Assaults	10	9	–	3	22
Robbery/theft from person	6	–	–	5	11
Vehicle vandalism	–	4	6	6	16
Vehicle thefts	<1	2	5	5	13
ALL BCS OFFENCES	14	4	2	3	22
ALL BCS INCIDENTS					
Personal thefts	51	4	1	1	56
Threats	16	3	<1	1	21
Assaults	7	6	–	2	15
Robbery/theft from person	5	–	–	6	11
Vehicle vandalism	–	4	4	5	13
Vehicle thefts	–	2	4	4	11
ALL BCS OFFENCES	9	3	1	2	15

Notes:

1. Personal thefts comprise: theft of personal property away from the home – with no contact between victim and offender. Assaults comprise: common assault, wounding, and sexual offences. Sexual offences are very small in number. Vehicle thefts include theft of and from cars and motorbikes, and attempts, base vehicle owners.
2. Based on all incidents during recall period analysed in the Victim Form.
3. Weighted data. Source: 1988 BCS (core sample).

Table A.12
Occupations with above average job-related risks: categories from the Condensed Key Occupations for Statistical Purposes

Category	Order	Code	Occupations
EDUCATION/WELFARE/HEALTH			
Higher education	Order 2,	010	Teachers in higher education
Teachers	Order 2,	011	Teachers n.e.c.
Welfare workers	Order 2,	013	Matrons, houseparents; playgroup leaders; welfare occupations n.e.c.
Medical and dental practitioners	Order 2,	015	
Nurses	Order 2,	016	Nurse administrators, nurses
LITERARY/ARTISTIC/SPORTS			
All the category	Order 3,	019	Authors, writers, journalists
		020	Artists, designers window dressers
		021	Actors, musicians, entertainers, stage managers
		022	Photographers, cameramen, sound and vision equipment operators
		023	All other literary, artistic and sports
MANAGERIAL (1)			
Production and site managers	Order 5,	034	Production, works and maintenance managers, works foremen
		035	Site and other managers, agents and clerks of work, general foremen
Office managers	Order 5,	037	Office managers (credit controllers, office managers n.e.c.)
Retail and wholesale	Order 5,	038	Managers in wholesale and retail distribution (garage proprietors, butchers, fishmongers, other proprietors and managers (sales)
Entertainment managers	Order 5	039	Managers of hotels, clubs etc, and in entertainment and sport (hotel and residential club managers, publicans, restauranteurs, club stewards, entertainment and sports managers
Security	Order 5,	043	Senior police, prison and fire service officers
	Order 8,	060	Supervisors (police sergeants, fire fighting and related)
		061	Policemen, firemen, prison officers
		062	Other security and protective service workers
SELLING			
Sales reps	Order 7,	057	Sales representatives and agents (importers, etc); market and street traders; scrap dealers, etc; credit agents, collector salesmen; sales representatives, sales representatives (property and services), other agents
PERSONAL SERVICES			
Waitresses and bar staff	Order 9,	065	Waiters, waitresses; barmen, barmaids
Housekeeping and related	Order 9,	067	Supervisors – housekeeping and related (housekeepers (non-domestic)); supervisors of domestic and school helpers, hospital porters, hotel porters, ambulancemen, hospital ward orderlies)
		069	Travel stewards and attendants, hospital and hotel porters

Table A.13
Membership of Neighbourhood Watch schemes, by region

	Scheme set up	*Take-up rate where schemes set up*	*Members of schemes as % of total sample*
	%	%	%
HIGH COVERAGE REGIONS			
North West	29	87	23
South East	28	77	19
Northern	24	79	16
West Midlands	21	81	15
LOW COVERAGE REGIONS			
Yorkshire and Humberside	9	63	5
South West	8	77	5
East Midlands	9	58	4
East Anglia	7	73	4
Wales	6	62	2
NATIONAL AVERAGE	20	78	14

Note:
1. Weighted data. Source: 1988 BCS, core sample.

Table A.14
General crime prevention activities among members and non-members

	Members of NW	*Non-members*
	% of households who had:	
A security survey by the police	10	4
Marked bicycles with post code	16	9
Marked household property	33	12
Told neighbour times when home empty	66	58

Note:
1. Weighted data. Source: 1988 BCS, core sample.

Table A.15
Perceived benefits of Neighbourhood Watch schemes

	% mentioning
People's homes are watched	41
Deters crime	38
Increases awareness of risk of being victim	16
Improves neighbourliness	13
Makes people safer/feel safer	11
Keeps young people out of trouble	1
Helps police	2

Note:
1. Weighted data. Source: 1988 BCS, core sample.

Table A.16
Perceived burglary risk for members and non-members of Neighbourhood Watch, within ACORN neighbourhood group

	Non-members	*Members*	*Difference*
	% saying burglary 'likely' in next year		
A. Agricultural areas	19	23	+ 4
C. Older housing of intermediate status	24	34	+10
K. Better-off retirement areas	19	38	+19
J. Affluent suburban areas	26	38	+12
B. Modern family housing, higher incomes	24	28	+ 4
E. Better-off council estates	27	39	+12
D. Poor quality older terraced housing	31	39	+ 8
F. Less well-off council estates	31	46	+15
I. High-status non-family areas	32	37	+ 5
H. Multi-racial areas	37	59	+22
G. Poorest council estates	43	35	– 8
NATIONAL AVERAGE	27	35	+ 8

Notes:
1. The % 'saying burglary is likely next year' is based on those who said they were 'certain to' or 'very likely' to have a burglary.
2. Weighted data. Source: 1988 BCS, core sample.

Appendix B
Multivariate analysis, Chapters 5 and 6

The method of logistic regression of LOGIT analysis is a multivariate statistical technique which allows the assessment of the effect of various independent variables simultaneously. It thus reveals whether any independent variable (eg ethnicity or age) known or thought to be important in explaining the dependent variable (eg, the risk of threats) is statistically related to it once any possible association with other variables has been taken into account. For example, age and marital status are both related to the risk of being threatened, but they are also related to each other (older people are more likely to be married). A LOGIT analysis would say whether age has any effect on risk on its own that is not simply explained by the association between marital status and risk.

When dealing with dichotomous dependent variables and categorical independent variables (as we are here), LOGIT is the most appropriate multivariate approach. For each independent variable there is a 'reference' category with which the remaining categories are compared. For instance, in Table B.1 the category of those 30 or under is the reference category and those over 30 are compared with younger people (who are otherwise comparable to them on the other independent variables). The size of each 'estimate' in the table is a measure of how different that category is from the reference category – with regard to the dependent variable. The direction of the sign indicates the direction of the difference. In Table B.1, for example, those over 30 are less likely than younger people to be threatened (we know this from the negative sign). We know that the difference is significant as the estimate divided by the standard error gives a significant t-ratio. For a detailed explanation of the use of LOGIT analysis see Box *et al.* (1988).

Table B.1
Maximum likelihood estimates of the coefficients in the LOGIT model: Threats: Whites and Asians

	Estimate	*S.E*	*t Ratio*	*Sig*
	DEPENDENT VARIABLE:		*% victim of threats over the recall period*	
Constant	-3.1690	0.1840	-17.2	*
2nd Residential scale	0.7906	0.1374	5.8	*
Sex – women	-0.7205	0.1317	-5.5	*
Manual workers	-0.6097	0.1268	-4.8	*
Aged over 30	-0.6163	0.1420	-4.3	*
Not married	0.3016	0.1383	2.2	*
Asian	0.2409	0.1946	1.2	

	D.F	Deviance
Residual	57	65.080

Notes:
1. Strictly, design effects (see Appendix D) as well as sampling error should be taken into account in calculating t ratios. Asterisked t ratios are significant at the 5% probability level, though it should be borne in mind that marginally significant values may be a little suspect as design effects have not been accounted for.
2. The residential stability scale is composed of four variables too highly correlated to be included separately. It was derived using principal components analysis from neighbourhood cohesion, time respondent has lived in the area, likelihood of moving from the area and housing condition. The scale values were dichotomised at the mean. See also note 4, Table B.2.
3. Unweighted data. Source: 1988 BCS (core sample).

Table B.2
Maximum likelihood estimates of the coefficients in the LOGIT model: Vandalism: Whites and Asians

	Estimate	*S.E*	*t-Ratio*	*Sig*
	DEPENDENT VARIABLE:		*% victim of vandalism over the recall period*	
Constant	–2.881	0.08502	–33.9	*
High incivilities	0.8261	0.07561	10.9	*
Residential stability scale	0.4121	0.06351	6.5	*
Higher than average income	0.4463	0.07757	5.8	*
Did not specify income	0.1895	0.08416	2.3	*
Council and private renters	–0.6710	0.1644	–4.1	*
Council and private renters – incivilities interaction	0.5225	0.1803	2.9	*
Asian	0.2598	0.09969	2.6	*
D.F Deviance				
Residual 40 40.399				

Notes:
1. See note 1 to Table B.l.
2. A third level was included for the income variable to include cases where income information was refused. This was d on e to avoid losing too many cases through missing data.
3. The measure of incivilities is the same as that used by Box *et al.* (1988) – an index constructed from answers to five questions on perceived levels of litter, grafitti, teenagers hanging around street corners, noisy parties, and drunks and tramps in the neighbourhood.
4. The second residential stability scale is derived in exactly the same way as the first, except that incivilites is included in the scale with the four other variables. The scale values were again dichotomised at the mean.
5. 'Private renters' includes those renting from housing associations and cases where the property was tied to the job.
6. Unweighted data. Source: 1988 BCS (core sample).

Table B.3
Maximum likelihood estimates of the coefficients in the LOGIT model:
Robbery and theft from the person: Whites and Asians

	Estimate	*S.E*	*t Ratio*	*Sig*
	DEPENDENT VARIABLE:		*% victim of robbery and theft from the person over the recall period*	
Constant	–5.192	0.1589	–32.7	*
Inner city residents	0.8991	0.1721	5.2	*
Asian	0.8551	0.2164	4.0	*
Not married	0.6445	0.1689	3.8	*
Council and private renters	0.4809	0.1718	2.8	*
Unemployed	0.4283	0.1933	2.2	*

	D.F	Deviance
Residual	57	63.091

Notes:
1. See note 1 to Table B.1 and note 5 to Table B.2.
2. The unemployed category includes all those out of work and seeking work at some time over the recall period.
3. Unweighted data. Source: 1988 BCS (core sample).

Table B.4
Maximum likelihood estimates of the coefficients in the LOGIT model:
Burglary: Whites and Afro-Caribbean

	Estimate	*S.E*	*t Ratio*	*Sig*
	DEPENDENT VARIABLE:		*% victim of burglary over the recall period*	
Constant	–3.451	0.1193	–28.9	*
Household head aged over 40	–0.6461	0.09120	–7.1	*
High incivilities	0.6134	0.09878	6.2	*
Inner City residents	0.5458	0.09614	5.7	*
High risk area	0.5190	0.09746	5.3	*
Sex of HH head – women	0.4629	0.09819	4.7	*
Residential scale	0.2890	0.09391	3.1	*
Afro-Caribbean	–0.2064	0.1469	–1.4	

	D.F	Deviance
Residual	120	121.71

Notes:
1. See notes 1 and 2 to Table B.1 and note 3 to Table B.2.
2. High risk areas include acorn groups D, E, F, G, H, and I.
3. Unweighted data. Source: 1988 BCS (core sample).

Table B.5
Maximum likelihood estimates of the coefficients in the LOGIT model: Assault: Whites and Afro-Caribbean

	Estimate	*S.E*	*t Ratio*	*Sig*
	DEPENDENT VARIABLE:		*% victim of assault over the recall period*	
Constant	–3.201	0.2129	–15.0	*
Aged over 30	–1.764	0.2656	–6.6	*
Sex – women	–0.6156	0.1154	–5.3	*
Not married	0.7659	0.1717	4.5	*
Evenings outside home	0.3798	0.1192	3.2	*
2nd Residential scale	0.4570	0.1588	2.9	*
Unemployed	0.3594	0.1416	2.5	*
Age – scale interaction	0.6898	0.2656	2.6	*
Age – unemployment interaction	0.6395	0.2722	2.3	*
Age – not married interaction	–0.6134	0.2752	–2.2	*
Afro-Caribbean	0.2393	0.1655	1.4	

	D.F	Deviance
Residual	117	130.03

Notes:
1. See note 1 to Table B.1, note 4 to Table B.2 and note 2 to Table B.3.
2. The reference category for evenings outside the home includes those who went out for either none or only one evening in the previous week.
3. Unweighted data. Source: 1988 BCS (core sample).

Table B.6
Maximum likelihood estimates of the coefficients in the LOGIT model: Robbery and theft from the person: Whites and Afro-Caribbean

	Estimate	*S.E*	*t Ratio*	*Sig*
	DEPENDENT VARIABLE:		*% victim of robbery and theft from the person over the recall period*	
Constant	–5.008	0.2335	–21.4	*
Inner city residents	1.034	0.1808	5.7	*
Aged over 30	–0.6011	0.1785	–3.4	*
Sex – women	0.4893	0.1757	2.8	*
Council and private renters	0.5089	0.1778	2.9	*
Not married	0.4987	0.1861	2.7	*
Afro-Caribbean	0.1707	0.2391	0.7	

	D.F	Deviance
Residual	57	53.956

Notes:
1. See notes 1 and 5 to Table B.2.
2. Unweighted data. Source: 1988 BCS (core sample).

Table B.7
Maximum likelihood estimates of the coefficients in the LOGIT model: NW membership

	Estimate	*S.E*	*t Ratio*	*Sig*
	DEPENDENT VARIABLE:		*Membership of NW*	
High-risk area	–0.641	0.080	–8.011	*
Higher than average income	0.561	0.088	6.404	*
Council renters	–0.852	0.182	–4.688	*
Private renters	–0.370	0.216	-1.713	
31-60 age group	0.442	0.106	4.179	*
61+ age group	0.553	0.117	4.746	*
Council renters/high-risk area interaction	0.465	0.201	2.312	*
Private renters/high-risk area interaction	0.765	0.249	3.075	*
Council renters/high-income interaction	–0.662	0.297	–2.229	*
Private renters/high-income interaction	–0.583	0.293	–1.992	*
D.F Deviance				
Residual 40 47.891				

Notes:
1. See note 1 to Table B.1.
2. A third level was included for the income variable to include cases where income information was refused. This was done to avoid losing too many cases through missing data. Results for this term are not shown.
3. High-risk areas include acorn groups D, E, F, G, H, and I.
4. 'Private renters' includes those renting from housing associations and cases where the property was tied to the job.
5. Unweighted data. Source: 1988 BCS (core sample).

Table B.4
Maximum likelihood estimates of the coefficients in the LOGIT model: Worry about burglary

	Estimate	*S.E*	*t Ratio*	*Sig*
	DEPENDENT VARIABLE:		*% very and fairly worried about burglary*	
Low perceived risk	–1.707	0.124	–13.777	*
Low Incivilities	–0.561	0.061	–9.216	*
Previous victim	0.299	0.047	6.481	*
Sex – Women	0.267	0.054	4.962	*
High area crime rate	0.196	0.043	4.543	*
Member of NW	0.238	0.060	3.985	*
Incivilities-sex interaction	0.166	0.083	1.999	*

	D.F	Deviance
Residual	56	56.314

Notes:
1. See note 1 to Table B.1.
2. The measure of incivilities is the same as that used by Box *et al.* (1988) – an index constructed from answers to five questions on perceived levels of litter, graffiti, teenagers hanging around street corners, noisy parties, and drunks and tramps in the neighbourhood.
3. The measure of 'area crime' was the same as that used by Maxfield (1987). The average number of victimisations was calculated for all persons living in each sampling unit. This was then dichotomised on either side of the overall mean into 'low' and 'high' crime areas.
4. Unweighted data. Source: 1988 BCS (core sample).

Appendix C
Survey design and methods

The coverage of the survey

The BCS aims not only to estimate crime levels, but to provide a range of extra information on matters related to crime. In addition to demographic information, the 1988 questionnaire covered the following main topics:

a. the extent and nature of household and personal victimisation;

b. the extent of verbal abuse at work;

c. fear of crime and perceptions of risk;

d. contacts with the police;

e. drinking behaviour and drunken driving;

f. attitudes to sentencing;

g. membership of, and attitudes to Neighbourhood Watch schemes;

h. security behaviour in relation to burglary and autocrime;

i. household fires.

To ensure comparability, most questions on victimisation (a. above) were the same as in the 1982 and 1984 surveys. Questions on the extent of verbal abuse at work (b. above) were included in the survey at the request of the Health and Safety Executive. Fear of crime was dealt with less extensively than in the. 1984 survey. The questions on contacts with the police were extensive, and many of them were new to the 1988 survey (see Skogan, forthcoming, for results). Questions on drunken driving were broadly similar to those in previous surveys. Many questions under f., g. and h. above were new to the 1988 survey. The coverage of household fires was also new to the BCS. By no means all the results from the survey have been presented in this report, and further publications are scheduled.

There were four parts of the questionaire: the *Main Questionnaire;* the *Victim Form;* the *Follow-up Questionnaire;* and the *Demographic Questionnaire.* There were two versions of the *Follow-up Questionnaire,* one of which concentrated on the police, the other on items e. to i. above.

Whilst every respondent completed the Main, Demographic and one or other version of the Follow-up Questionnaires, only victims completed Victim Forms (up to a limit of four). (The largely attitudinal questions in the two Follow-up Questionnaires did not require the same precision as those in other parts, so the sample was reduced.) There were two versions of the Main Questionnaire; half of all Main Questionnaires required Victim Forms to be completed when respondents reported experience of vandalism; the other half did not. (This was done – given the frequency of incidents of vandalism - to reduce interviewer workloads and costs.)

Those victims answering all four parts of the questionnaire were interviewed on average for an hour; non-victims were interviewed for about 40 minutes.

Sampling

The 1988 BCS covered two groups: a 'core' sample and a 'booster' sample of ethnic minorities.

Core sample

The BCS core sample was designed to give, after appropriate weighting, a representative cross-section of people aged 16 and over living in private households whose addresses appear in the electoral register. People living in institutions were not sampled.

The electoral register was the sampling frame in the 1982 and 1984 surveys, and this was chosen again notwithstanding that it has been established that registers do not cover all private households – about 4% are omitted, in particular those with young people, the unemployed, ethnic minorities and those in rented accomodation (Todd and Butcher, 1982). Methods are available to fill the gaps, but as these are of questionable reliability and pose difficulties for interviewers, no use was made of them. Serious consideration was given to a more complete and unbiased sampling frame – the Post Office's Postcode Address File (PAF). However, PAF would had added considerably to the complexity of interpreting *changes* in victimisation rates between the 1988 survey and previous sweeps. Costs would also have been higher in that about 12% of non-residential and ineligible PAF addresses would have needed to be screened out.

The sampling for the survey was in five stages, and matched procedures used in the 1984 survey:

i. selection of parliamentary constituencies;

ii. selection of wards within these constituencies;

iii. selection of polling districts;

iv. selection of addresses; and

v. selection of individuals for interview at these addresses.

i. Selection of constituencies

300 of the 561 constituencies in England and Wales were selected for sampling, the same constituences as in 1984. Because of high crime levels in inner city areas, these were sampled in higher proportion than their population would justify. In the 1982 survey, inner city areas were identified through the PRAG classification of parliamentary constituencies (see Hough and Mayhew, 1983: 38). A different procedure was adopted for the design of the 1984 survey as the PRAG classification was by then some 13 years out of date and 1983 Boundary revisions had altered the composition of constituencies. In the 1988 survey, as in 1984, inner city constituencies were rather more widely defined than in 1982 as those:

i. With a high population density. (The 1982 survey's 59 PRAG inner-city constituencies converted to 53 new constituencies. Taking all constituencies with a population density equal to or above that of the lowest in the converted 1982 PRAG inner-city constituencies gave 177 constituencies).

ii. In towns above a certain size. (The minimum town size was set at 200,000 total population, reducing the number of constituencies to 155).

iii. Having at least one of two other typical inner-city characteristics: low levels of owner-occupation and a low social class profile. (Of the 155 constituencies, 50 were ruled out on grounds of being higher than the national average on either owner-occupation or social class. This eliminated 4 of the original 53 constituencies which matched the 1982 inner-city ones.)

At the time of the 1984 survey, the 105 inner-city constituencies contained 17.9% of the total electorate and these were to be represented at 1.5 times the proportion its electorate would justify, being allocated 79 of the 300 constituencies to be selected. The same allocation was made for the 1988 survey. Further stratification of the sample was carried out on the basis of the nine Registrar General's Standard regions, population density and socio-economic group. All constituencies were selected with a probability proportional to their size.

ii. Selection of wards

Within the selected constituencies, additional clustering of the sample was required and two wards were selected within each constituency, again with a probability proportional to the electorate. The wards were the same as in 1984.

iii. Selection of polling districts

The final sampling units, from which names and addresses were drawn, was one of polling districts in each ward. Because polling districts within wards are fairly homogeneous, it was not felt necessary to select polling districts at probability proportional to size. One polling district was selected per ward; local electoral registration offices were asked to supply the last polling district in alphabetical or numerical order for each of the two wards selected. (In 1984, the *first* polling district was asked for.)

iv. Selection of addresses

23 names were drawn in each polling district, yielding an issued sample of 13,800. A random start point was chosen and every fifteenth name was underlined, until 23 names had been selected. (People living at addresses which were obviously institutions were excluded.)

v. Selection of individuals for interview

The final stage of sampling, the selection of individuals at addresses for interview, was carried out by interviewers in the field. Institutional or non-residential addresses were eliminated first. Where there were two or more households at the address, the interviewer sought out the household which included the elector on whose account the address was chosen, or the household now occupying the part of the accommodation where that person used to live. Where this could be done, the interviewer treated that household as the unit for interview; if it could not, the entire address was treated as a single unit.

Within each household, the interviewer then established whether all the relevant electors were still living there and whether there was anyone else in the household aged 16 or over. If all the electors still lived there and no other person aged 16 or over was present, an interview was sought with the person on whose account the address was selected. If either of these conditions did not apply, the interviewer listed all persons aged 16 or over currently in the household and chose one for interview using a random selection grid.

To represent the population aged 16 and over living in private households at addresses listed in the electoral registers, corrections had to be made to the sample at the data-processing stage to correct for:

i. the oversampling of inner city areas; and

ii. cases where the number of electors, which has been used as a proxy for the number of persons aged 16 or over, and the actual number of persons of this age did not match.

Further details of the weighting of data are given below.

Ethnic minority 'booster' sample

As no systematic listing of ethnic minority groups exists, procedures for choosing respondents for the booster sample were necessarily different. The method of focussed enumeration was chosen (see Brown and Ritchie, 1981) to give a representative cross-section of people who were of Black or Asian origin. Basically, this involved the interviewer, at each address in the main example, 'screening' a number of adjacent addresses by asking separately for each of these addresses whether there was 'anyone living at (. . . six adjacent addresses . . .) who is black or is of Asian origin'. (If no answer could be got from the main address, the question could be posed to householders at the adjacent addresses themselves.) Interviewers then went on to try and conduct an interview at each address at which a Black or Asian householder was said to be living, having first chosen – on a random basis – which person should be interviewed from all those aged 16 or more living in the household.

Based on Census data, other population estimates, and previous research experience, it was felt best to 'screen' six addresses to generate interviews with 1,700 ethnic minority respondents. ('Screening' questions were asked about three addresses to the left and three to the right, with specific instructions being laid down for interviews where residential layout did not allow this to be done simply (see NOP/SCPR, 1989).

Within the booster sample, 'blacks' will cover Afro-Caribbeans or Africans. Asians are those who classified themselves as Indian, Pakistani or Bangladeshi (In the event, a small number of booster sample respondents put themselves into the category of 'Chinese', 'other Asian', or 'other'; these have been omitted from analysis, as they would not necessarily be representative of these groups.)

All respondents in the booster sample completed Follow-Up B questionnaires (on policing) – since one reason for oversampling ethnic minorities was to see if their experience of the police differed from those of whites.

Some comparisons are made in this report of 'whites', 'blacks' and 'Asians'. For this purpose, ethnic minority respondents in the core sample who called themselves Black, Indian, Pakistani or Bangladeshi (the groups the booster sample was meant to pick up) are added to the boost sample. A small number of respondents who fell into other ethnic groups (including Chinese and other Asian) are excluded from comparisons.

Fieldwork

Of the issued sample of 13,800 addresses in the core sample, 2.7% were empty, demolished, or ineligible for interview for other reasons. The remaining 13,433 addresses yielded 10,392 achieved interviews, a response rate of 77.4%. At 50% of the addresses where no successful interview took place, the selected respondent refused to be interviewed; non-contact accounted for most of the other failures. The response rate was 71.3% in inner-cities, 79.4% elsewhere.

Response rates were very similar to the 1984 survey; in 1982, response rates were fractionally higher.

A total of 328 interviewers worked on the 1988 BCS. 49% of successful interviews with those in the core sample had taken place by the end of February, 1988; 43% took place in March, and 7% later than this. A small number of interviews were undated.

Interviews with the booster sample ran a little later. 28% of successful interviews had taken place by the end of February, 49% took place in March, and 21% later than this. Again, a small number of interviews were undated.

In the booster sample, 2,254 addresses were positively screened, at which an interview was achieved at 1,349 – a response rate of 59.8%. Rather more respondents in the booster sample (15%) refused to be interviewed than in the core sample (11%). Also, more in the booster sample were not contacted after repeated calls, or were not interviewed because of language difficulties.

Representativeness of the samples

The characteristics and representativeness of those interviewed in the core sample are described in the survey's Technical Report (NOP/SCPR, 1989). In general, the representativeness of the core sample was sound. However, as regards age, there was a slight shortfall among men and women in 16-29 age group, with a compensatory increase among those in middle-age groups (see Table C.1).

Table C.1
Percentage of respondents in different age/sex groups: core sample

	Men 16-29	*Men* 30-44	*Men* 45+	*Men*	*Women* 16-29	*Women* 30-44	*Women* 45+	*Women*	*TOTAL* over 16
Population aged 16 or more									
OPCS 1987 estimates	14.1	12.9	21.1	48.1	13.7	12.8	25.4	51.9	100.0
BCS core sample	11.8	13.2	23.4	48.4	12.1	14.4	25.1	51.6	100.0

Notes:
1. OPCS figures are mid-year estimates for the 1987 England and Wales population aged 16 or more.
2. BCS: weighted data; unweighted n = 10,392. Source: 1988 BCS, core sample.

As the 1981 Census did not measure ethnicity, there are no comprehensive data on the numbers of people in different ethnic groups against which the representativeness of the BCS sample can be compared. However, some information on ethnicity is available from the large-scale Labour Force Survey (LFS). Although this survey will be subject to similar response biases as the BCS (eg, it is likely to under-represent young people), a comparison is nonetheless useful of whether the coverage of the selected ethnic minority groups in the BCS was reasonably in line with results from the LFS. Table C.2 compares the age and sex distribution of those interviewed in the LFS with the two ethnic minority groups interviewed in the BCS core and booster samples. Proportionately more Asian men were picked up in the BCS, and fewer elderly Asian women. The distribution by age and sex of Afro-Caribbeans/Africans interviewed in the two surveys is similar. It can be noted that compared to England and Wales as a whole (Table C.1), ethnic minorities are a younger population as measured by both the BCS and LFS.

Table C.2
Percentage of ethnic minority respondents in different age/sex groups: BCS and Labour Force Survey compared

	Men 16-29	*Men 30-44*	*Men 45+*	*Men*	*Women 16-29*	*Women 30-44*	*Women 45+*	*Women*	*Total over 16*
Afro-Caribbeans and Africans									
LFS	20.6	10.2	17.1	47.9	23.9	13.4	14.8	52.1	100.0
BCS	20.1	11.3	15.3	46.8	23.1	16.7	13.4	53.2	100.0
Asians									
LFS	19.3	17.1	15.3	51.6	21.7	15.7	11.0	48.7	100.0
BCS	21.2	20.8	18.0	60.0	19.7	13.6	6.7	40.0	100.0
Both groups									
LFS	19.8	14.6	16.0	50.4	22.5	14.8	12.4	49.6	100.0
BCS	20.8	17.5	17.1	54.4	20.9	14.7	9.0	45.6	100.0

Notes:
1. LFS figures calculated from Shaw, 1988, with an adjustment made for ethnic minorities in England and Wales only. The ethnic groups counted are Afro-Caribbeans/Africans; Indians, Pakistani, and Bangladeshi. Figures are based on averages from the 1984-1986 surveys. Each year, some 150,000 individuals were interviewed from about 60,000 households.
2. BCS: weighted data; unweighted n = 1,736. Source: 1988 BCS, core and boost samples.

Weighting

Data from the survey were weighted in a number of ways at the data processing stage. Weighting served two main purposes: to correct imbalances introduced in sampling; and to correct imbalances created by the design of the interview. Weights were applied to correct for the following:

i. The inner city imbalance: taking actual contacts rates into account, inner city areas were effectively oversampled by a factor of 1.39.

ii. The mismatch between electors and persons at addresses when data were used to represent the adult population: each record was weighted by a factor of a/e, where a was the number of persons 16 or over living in the household and e was the number of electors relevant to that household. In most cases, the numbers matched and the weight was one.

iii. Household crimes: for crimes (eg, burglary) where the victim is the household rather than the individual respondent, each record was weighted by a factor of 1/e, where e was the number of electors relevant to the household. A weight of less than 1 was applied to most of the sample.

iv. Victim incidents: where it was necessary to produce tabulations for victim incidents in general (ie, both personal and household crimes), personal victim incidents were weighted by ii. above and household victim incidents by iii above.

v. Series offences: for series offences (see below), only a single Victim Form was completed. In the analysis of victim incidents, these forms were weighted by the number of incidents involved, with an arbitrary top limit of five.

The omission of damage victim forms

Victim Forms were completed for instances of vandalism (criminal damage) for only a randomly selected half of respondents who gave positive answers to the appropriate screening. As was the case in 1984, allowance was made for the omission of damage forms in the 1988 survey by imputation rather than weighting. This was regarded as a more efficient form of correction than that employed in the 1982 survey. (Full details of the imputation process are given in the Technical Report (NOP/SCPR, 1989). In analysis of Victim Forms, those originating from vandalism 'screeners' were double weighted.

Series victimisations

When a person is victim of a number of very similar offences, it is not always possible for him/her to separate them into discrete events. In an already lengthy interview, it is also very demanding for respondents to report on all the incidents separately. Offences of this kind are usually called *series incidents*. In the BCS, interviewers could treat incidents as a series provided that they were all very similar in type, were done under the same circumstances and probably committed by the same person(s).

For crimes classified as series offences, full details were collected only about the most recent incident. In calculating offence rates for 1987, series incidents were given a score equal to the number of incidents in the series occurring in 1987, with an arbitrary top limit of five.

Classifying and counting incidents

Incidents were classified by SCPR coders with each Victim Form being given one of more than 50 offence codes. Virtually the same set of instructions for classifying incidents were used as in the 1982 and 1984 BCS, though a few small changes were introduced in the rules for classifying threats, assaults, and thefts from the person. The classifying rules for the BCS were drawn up in consultation with the Home Office Statistical Department and with the statistics branches of a number of police forces, so as to enable comparison with statistics of offences recorded by the police. A number of incidents in the survey (7%) for which Victim Forms were completed were not included in any of the analyses of offences, for instance, because they fell outside the survey's coverage (eg, burglary of business premises) or because there was insufficient evidence that an offence had occurred. Victim Forms were completed for incidents of threatening behaviour though, for the most part, these have not been included in analyses of offences in this report; threats comprised 5% of legitimate BCS offences.

Respondents were interviewed in early 1988, and asked about incidents which had happened since 1 January 1987. In calculating offence rates for 1987 all incidents occurring in 1988 were excluded; incidents other than series incidents (see above) were counted once (prior to weighting), and series incidents were given a score equal to the number of incidents in the series occurring in 1987, with an arbitrary top limit of five.

Appendix D
Sampling error

A sample is a small-scale representation of the population from which it is drawn. Survey estimates of characteristics of the population are subject to imprecision because of both sampling and non-sampling error. For example, an estimate of household income might be inaccurate because the sample failed to reflect the parent population adequately (sampling error) or because respondents provided inaccurate information to interviewers (a form of non-sampling error). Various sorts of non-sampling error have been discussed in Chapter 1.

The estimates in this report are based on a sample of the population in England and Wales aged 16 or over. The sample matches the national profile well, though there were 2% fewer 16-19 year olds in the sample than in the population at large (NOP/SCPR, 1989), and institutionalised respondents were excluded: both these groups may be disproportionately victimised. This apart, the sample may well produce estimates which differ slightly from figures which would have been obtained if the whole population had been interviewed. One measure of the likely difference is given by the standard error, which indicates the extent to which an estimate might have varied by chance because only a sample was interviewed. The chances are about 68 in a 100 that a sample estimate will differ by less than one standard error from the figure which would have been obtained in a complete census of the population, and about 95 in a 100 that the difference would be less than two standard errors.

Tables D.1 and D.2 present errors for a selection of BCS statistics for the 'core' and 'booster' samples respectively. The Simple Random Sample (SRS) standard errors are estimates of the sampling error which a simple random sample of the size of the BCS would have achieved. The BCS did not employ a simple random sample, however, but used clustering, stratification and weighting (as described in Appendix C). The complex standard errors take account of these factors. Deft or $\sqrt{deff}$ is the ratio of the complex standard error to the SRS standard error. Defts were calculated by NOP, using the method of Balanced Repeated Replications (see NOP/SCPR), 1989).

The numbers of various offences in England and Wales, used in Chapter 2, are derived by multiplying rates per 10,000 by the number of households (for household offences) and by the population over the age of 16. The multipliers, respectively, were 1927.3000 and 4013.7000 (see Appendix E for further details). The range within which the number of offences lies can be calculated from the statistics in Table D.1 (eg, with 95% certainty the number of incidents of vandalism will fall between 2,687,000 and 3,176,00.

Table D.2
Sampling errors for selected BCS statistics: 'booster' sample

	Rate	*SRS st. error*	*Complex st. error*	*'Deft' ($\sqrt{deff}$)*
Rates per 10,000 households				
Vandalism	2183	199	179	0.90
Theft from vehicle	1079	118	150	1.27
Burglary	868	108	130	1.20
Theft of vehicle	295	49	76	1.54
Bicycle theft	113	30	30	0.97
Theft in a dwelling	78	30	27	0.91
Other household theft	950	124	135	1.09
All household offences	5568	309	374	1.21
Rates per 10,000 adults				
Wounding	198	51	54	1.05
Common assault	338	67	94	1.40
Assault	536	84	126	1.50
Theft from the person	209	45	40	0.90
Robbery	94	29	32	1.12
Theft from person/robbery	304	53	97	1.84
Sexual offences	23	24	16	0.65
Other personal theft	272	48	77	1.60
All personal offences	1122	114	170	1.49
Other rates				
Theft from vehicle (owners)	1699	181	226	1.25
Theft of vehicle (owners)	465	76	96	1.27
Bicycle theft (owners)	311	86	94	1.09
Classified as Afro-Caribbean	33.8%	1.29%	2.93%	2.27
Classified as Asian	66.2%	1.29%	2.96%	2.29

Notes.
1. Incidence rates are those presented in Table 1, Appendix A. Rates for sexual offences are per 10,000 women.
2. Weighted data; unweighted n = 1,349, or slightly less for 'other rates' where there are missing values. Source: 1988 BCS, booster sample.

Table D.1
Sampling errors for selected BCS statistics: 'core' sample

	Rate	*SRS st. error*	*Complex st. error*	*'Deft' ($\sqrt{deff}$)*
Rates per 10,000 households				
Vandalism	1521	56	63	1.14
Theft from vehicle	1083	40	47	1.18
Burglary	612	31	40	1.30
Theft of vehicle	200	16	17	1.10
Bicycle theft	201	17	21	1.28
Theft in a dwelling	58	11	15	1.32
Other household theft	946	40	65	1.60
All household offences	4621	97	150	1.54
Rates per 10,000 adults				
Wounding	141	19	25	1.34
Common assault	372	31	35	1.14
Assault	513	38	45	1.20
Theft from the person	79	9	10	1.08
Robbery	44	9	10	1.08
Theft from person/robbery	124	13	14	1.07
Sexual offences	29	8	10	1.22
Other personal theft	447	27	34	1.26
All personal offences	1099	51	68	1.33
Other rates				
Theft from vehicle (owners)	1533	54	60	1.11
Theft of vehicle (owners)	282	21	23	1.09
Bicycle theft (owners)	451	35	48	1.38
Police knew about matter (victims)	36.6%	0.68%	0.91%	1.34
Feel 'unsafe' out alone	32.7%	0.46%	0.65%	1.41
Experienced verbal abuse at work	8.8%	0.28%	0.31%	1.10
Burglary screen =1 (Q29)	2.3%	0.16%	0.21%	1.34
Had fire in last 5 years	10.2%	0.41%	0.45%	1.10
Made 999 call to police	9.2%	0.41%	0.36%	0.87
Household in Neighbourhood Watch area	19.3%	0.57%	1.01%	1.77

Notes.
1. Incident rates are those presented in Table 1, Appendix A. Rates for sexual offences are per 10,000 women.
2. Weighted data; unweighted n = 10,392, or slightly less for 'other rates' where there are missing values. Source: 1988 BCS, core sample.

Appendix E
Comparison between the BCS and Criminal Statistics

Some offence groups can be compared using BCS information and offences recorded by the police as shown in *Criminal Statistics, England and Wales, 1987* (CS, see Home Office, 1988). For each of these, details are presented below on the precise offence categories which were compared. (The CS classification numbers are shown below in brackets after each relevant offence group.)

Survey offence rates for 1987 were grossed up to yield the number of offences likely to have been experienced in England and Wales in that year. To do this, household rates were multiplied by a factor of 1927.3000: 1987 household estimates from Department of the Environment, divided by 10,000. Personal rates were multiplied by a factor of 4013.7000: mid-1987 estimates for the number of persons over the age of 16 in England and Wales, divided by 10,000 (see OPCS, 1988). The household and personal multipliers used to derive numbers of offences in 1981 and 1983 are slightly different from those used in the presentation of previously published results from the 1982 and 1984 BCS in the respective overview reports (see Hough and Mayhew, 1983: 45; Hough and Mayhew, 1985: 85). The base of present 1981 and 1983 multipliers is more consistent with those available for 1987. They are: for 1981, 1819.5000 household, 3872.4100 personal; for 1983, they are 1844.3000 households, 3914.9000 personal.

Various adjustments were made to the CS categories of offences recorded by the police to account for instance for the fact that crimes against people under 16 appear in official records, but will not have been picked up in the survey.

These adjustments were largely the same as those made for comparison between results from the first BCS and offences recorded by the police in 1981. The 1988 adjustments were decided on the basis of information sent by 26 of the 43 police forces in England and Wales, and are thus only estimates. In 1988, a slightly different adjustment was made for sexual offences and bicycle thefts.

1. VANDALISM

Survey categories:

- Arson
- Criminal damage to motor vehicle, £20 or under
- Criminal damage to motor vehicle, over £20
- Criminal damage to the home, £20 or under
- Criminal damage to the home, over £20.

Criminal Statistics: Arson (56)
Criminal damage endangering life (excluding arson) (57)
Other indictable offences of criminal damage:
Value over £20 (58a)
Value £20 and under (58b)

Adjustments: i. The CS total of 587,878 is reduced to slightly more than a half – to 304,521 – to exclude offences committed against institutions and organisations.

2. THEFT FROM MOTOR VEHICLE

Survey categories: Theft from car/van
Theft from motorbike, motorscooter or moped

Criminal Statistics: Theft from vehicle (45)

Adjustments: i. The CS total of 658,577 is reduced by 5% to exclude attempted thefts, yielding 625,648.

Notes: i. No adjustment has been made to allow for the very small proportion of thefts from boats etc. recorded under the CS classification 45/11.

ii. No adjustment has been made to allow for the small proportion of thefts from commercial vehicles which would not be covered by the BCS.

3. THEFT OF MOTOR VEHICLE

Survey categories: Theft of car/van
Theft of motorbike, motorscooter or moped

Criminal Statistics: Theft and unauthorised taking of motor vehicle (48)

Adjustments: i. Attempted thefts are excluded from the comparison because of the difficulty of differentiating on the basis of BCS information between attempted thefts *of* and thefts *from* motor vehicles. The CS total of 389,576 is reduced by 5% to exclude attempted thefts, yielding 370,097.

ii. The figure of 370,097 yielded by i. has been reduced by 10% to exclude thefts of commercial vehicles, which would not have been covered by the BCS. The adjusted total is 333,087.

4. BURGLARY IN A DWELLING

Survey categories: Burglary in a dwelling (nothing taken)
Burglary in a dwelling (something taken)
Attempted burglary

Criminal Statistics: Burglary in a dwelling (28)
Aggravated burglary in a dwelling (29)

Adjustments: None

Notes i. The CS categories include attempts. In 22% of the total of CS burglaries there is "nil value" stolen; this may be slightly higher than the figure of burglaries where an attempt at entry only was made.

5. BICYCLE THEFT

Survey category: Theft of pedal cycle

Criminal Statistics: Theft of pedal cycle (44)

Adjustments i. Most police forces record incidents of bicycle theft as such, subsequently deleting or 'no crime-ing' the record if the bicycle is recovered. There is some doubt as to whether forces follow this procedure with any uniformity. The CS total of 119,445 is increased by 11% to include unauthorised takings recorded by the police and subsequently 'no-crimed' after the cycles' recovery. The adjusted total is 132,584. This adjustment is lower than the 15% used for CS figures for 1982 and 1984.

6. THEFT IN A DWELLING

Survey category: Theft in a dwelling

Criminal Statistics: Theft in a dwelling other than from automatic machine or meter (40)

Adjustments: None. The CS total is 46,550.

Notes: i. Thefts from meters in dwellings are classified separately in both CS and the survey.

7. SEXUAL OFFENCES

Survey categories: Rape
Attempted rape
Indecent assault

Criminal Statistics: Rape (19)
Indecent assault on a female (20)

Adjustments: i. To exclude cases where the victim was under the age of 16 (or mentally defective in the case of rape), the CS figure has been reduced by 38% from 15,811 to 9802. This reduction is larger than the 33% reduction made for CS figures for 1982 and 1984. Police returns indicate an increase in younger victims since 1984.

Notes: i. The CS category of rape includes attempts – perhaps around 10% of the total.

8. WOUNDING

Survey categories: Serious wounding
Other wounding
Serious wounding with sexual motive
Other wounding with sexual motive

Criminal Statisticts: Wounding or other act endangering life (5)
Other wounding, etc (8)

Adjustments: i. British Transport Police (BTP) keep their own crime statistics; these do not overlap in most cases with CS, but crimes for which there were prosecutions and very serious crimes tend to be included in the statistics maintained by local police forces. Thus, the 1382 cases of wounding which were recorded by the

BTP but not cleared up are added to the CS total of 137,135 to make 138,517.

ii. To exclude cases where the victim was under 16, the figure of 138,517 has been reduced by 15% to make 117,739.

9. ROBBERY

Survey categories: Robbery
Attempted robbery

Criminal Statistics: Robbery (34)

Adjustments:

i. The 1130 cases of robbery which were recorded by the BTP but not cleared up are added to the CS total of 32,633 to make 33,763.

ii. To exclude cases where the victim was under 16, the figure of 33,763 has been reduced by 12% to 29,711.

Notes:

i. Attempted robberies are classified by the police as robberies. They seem to amount to around 15%-20% of the total.

ii. About 25-30% of robberies recorded by the police involve business property – ie. post offices, banks, off-licences; an unknown proportion of these will have more than one victim. As the BCS assumes that there can be only one victim per robbery, there will be a slight tendency for the survey to overestimate the number of robberies – minimal enough to be disregarded. (It is assumed that virtually all robberies involving private property had single victims.)

10. THEFT FROM THE PERSON

Survey categories: Snatch theft from the person
Other theft from the person
Attempted theft from the person

Criminal Statistics: Theft from the person of another (39)

Adjustments:

i. The 8015 cases of theft from the person which were recorded by the BTP but not cleared up are added to the CS total of 33,535 to make 41,550.

ii. To exclude cases where the victim was under 16, the total of 41,550 has been reduced by 5% to 39,473.

Notes:

i. Attempted thefts from the person are classified by the police as thefts from the person, and probably amount to around 5-10% of the total.

Appendix F
Household burglary: comparing the BCS, the General Household Survey and offences recorded by the police

The General Household Survey (GHS) is an annual sample survey conducted by the Office of Population Censuses and Surveys of about 10,000 households in England and Wales. In 1972, 1973, 1979, 1980, 1985 and 1986, the GHS included questions, asked of the head of the household, to estimate the number of households which had been burgled in the last 12 months. The main question was: 'During the last 12 months (while you've been living here) has anyone got into this house/flat etc. without your permission and stolen or attempted to steal something?' Comparison of burglary trends between 1972 and 1980 as indicated by the GHS and statistics of recorded offences were presented in Home Office Statistical Bulletin No 11/82 (Home Office, 1982). An update on trends until 1983 was reported by Hough and Mayhew (1985: 16), and until 1985 by Elliott and Mayhew (1988).

Comparison of BCS and GHS burglary rates is not straightforward, for the following reasons:

i. The BCS definition of household burglary includes unsuccessful attempts to gain entry. Before 1985, the GHS asked only about incidents where the burglar effected entry, defining attempts as incidents where nothing was stolen. The 1985 and 1986, the GHS included a new question on attempted burglary, though for various technical reasons the comparison between GHS and BCS attempts is rather unsound.

ii. In the GHS, victims of burglary were taken to be those who answered in the affirmative to the question given above. There were no supplementary questions to check that the incident, as described by the respondent, met any specified criteria of burglary. In the BCS, the 'screen' question which was similar to the GHS question was used only to identify people who should be administered a Victim Form; incidents were then classified according to information given in the Victim Form. There may therefore be definitional differences in addition to i. above.

iii. Analysis of the GHS burglary questions excluded those who had moved to their home less than twelve months before interview.

The best comparison to make is between the GHS burglary rate (excluding incidents where nothing was taken, and in 1985 and 1986 attempts) and the response rate to the main burglary 'screen' questions in the BCS. In 1982 this was Question 22b of the Main Questionnaire, in 1984 Question 32. and in 1988 Question 29. However, the following adjustments had to be made to BCS data to enable valid comparison:

i. Excluded from analysis were those who had moved to their present home after the beginning of the respective recall period (eg, 1 January 1987 in the case of the 1988 survey). (The BCS shows that movers have higher burglary rates than others, so the burglary figures presented below are underestimates.) 'Movers' comprise about 10% of survey respondents.

ii. Any responses to the screen question which, according to the victim form, referred to incidents where nothing was taken were excluded.

iii. The relevant screen question was preceded by others concerned with theft and damage to cars, motor-bikes and bicycles; a few incidents which triggered responses to these screen questions were subsequently classified as burglaries, some of which would probably have triggered responses to the burglary screen, had this come first. Therefore, an arbitrary 50% of these incidents were added to the number of responses to the main burglary screen.

A further adjustment has to be made to GHS figures to improve comparability with the BCS. This is to account for differences in sampling. Sampling for the 1985 and 1986 GHS was from the Postcode Address File, whereas in previous years the Electoral Register was used (as in the BCS). The switch to PAF will give a more representative sample than the ER which is likely to undercount less stable households who could face higher-than-average burglary risks. There is no way of precisely estimating the effect of this on 1985 and 1986 GHS burglary risks, but previous work after the 1981 Census (Todd and Butcher, 1982) showed that about 4% of private households are missing from the ER. It has been assumed that (i) the ER shortfall is still an estimated 4%; (ii) PAF sampling picked up these 4% of households; and (iii) their burglary rate was 50% higher than households on the ER (a conservative estimate).

With these adjustments made, estimates of the number of burglaries with loss from the GHS for 1985 and 1986 and from the BCS for 1981, 1983 and 1987 are given below. In grossing up survey rates, the Inland Revenue's figure for the number of domestic rateable hereditaments in England and Wales has been used as the number of households in England and Wales – following practice in earlier analysis of the GHS findings. (The household figures used in the body of this report to analyse BCS rates are derived from projection based on the 1981 Census – see Appendix E. Some recoding changes to the 1981 and 1983 BCS data also alter the figures slightly from those previously published). The comparison must be regarded as tentative; not only are both figures subject to sampling and non-sampling error, but it is always problematic to compare findings from surveys with even small differences in design.

	BCS 1981	*BCS 1983*	*GHS 1985*	*GHS 1986*	*BCS 1987*
Burglary with loss	400,000 +/–70,000	431,000 +/–76,000	521,000 +/–79,000	479,000 +/–73,000	432,000 +/–76,000
Domestic rateable hereditaments (millions)	18.577	18.874	19.238	19.429	19.818

Note: The ranges of error for the BCS figures are approximate.

Burglaries with loss recorded by the police, which with BCS and GHS figures are compared in Figure 3 are all residential burglaries, minus nil–value cases. In years for which a GHS measure is given (eg, 1981), recorded offences refer to the average of the year of the survey and the previous year (eg 1981/80). This is because GHS respondents are interviewed throughout the survey year so that the 'recall period' for burglary will span the two years. (Figures shown in Hough and Mayhew, 1985: 17) are slightly different as an average was not used.) For other years, police figures relate to the calendar year.

It should be noted that in some comparisons of burglary as measured by the GHS and statistics of offences recorded by the police, the latter included both 'burglary in a dwelling' *and* 'theft in a dwelling' (see Home Office, 1982). The rationale for this was that although the GHS question was designed to identify burglary victims alone, it was thought that some respondents would have mistakenly reported incidents actually committed by non–trespassers. Here, as in previous comparisons of GHS and BCS results, the conclusion drawn about the increase in household burglaries as indicated by recorded offences on the one hand and by the GHS on the other refers only to burglaries in a dwelling; the GHS question has been assumed not to have identified incidents of theft from a dwelling. The justification for this was that the BCS screen question which corresponds most closely to the GHS question elicits very few incidents which, on the basis of Victim Form information, were subsequently classified as theft in a dwelling.

Appendix G
The Acorn system of area classification

ACORN stands for 'A Classification of Residential Neighbourhoods'. It is a system of classifying households according to the demographic, employment and housing characteristics of their immediate area. It was produced by CACI, a market and policy analysis consultancy, by applying the statistical technique of cluster analysis to variables from the 1981 Census. ACORN is now used for planning and marketing by a wide range of commercial and public sector organisations, and is being employed increasingly in social research.

There are 38 ACORN area types, these aggregating to 11 neighbourhood groups. Each of the 130,000 enumeration districts (EDs) in Great Britain (an average ED comprises about 150 households) has been assigned to an ACORN area type on the basis of its scores on 40 selected Census variables. As CACI have matched postcodes to enumeration districts, any household in the country can be given an ACORN code provided its full postcode is known.

The principle of ACORN is that people who live in the same neighbourhood share characteristics of class, income and lifestyle. Naturally, there will be differences between individual EDs within the same ACORN classification, and between households within the same ED – particularly in heterogeneous areas such as those in inner cities. Nevertheless, ACORN is a useful way of determining the immediate social environment of different households, and can be more illuminating for some purposes than individual characteristics such as income or class. For instance, ACORN will show what types of targets for crime different areas offer and what risks their residents face compared to those living nearby.

As was the case with the 1984 survey, each respondent in the 1988 BCS was allocated to an ACORN area type on the basis of the postcode for their address. The 11 neighbourhood groups were mainly used to analyse rates of victimisation, and other crime-related variables, such as fear, and membership of Neighbourhood Watch schemes. The BCS sample size is insufficient to make much use of the fuller 38 area types. The 11 ACORN groups are shown in Figure A, with the percentage of the 1987 England and Wales population in each group.

As Table G.1 shows, the distribution of households in the BCS sample across the different ACORN neighbourhood groups closely matches CACI's updates of the England and Wales figures for 1987. BCS respondents are slightly under-represented in group B (modern family housing, higher incomes) and slightly over-represented in group J (affluent suburban housing), but only to a small extent.

Figure A

ACORN Neighbourhood Groups

A

AGRICULTURAL AREAS

1 Agricultural villages
2 Areas of farms and smallholdings

3.4% of England and Wales households

B

MODERN FAMILY HOUSING, HIGHER INCOMES

3 Post-war functional private housing
4 Modern private housing, young families
5 Established private family housing
6 New detached houses, young families
7 Military bases

16.2% of England and Wales households

E

COUNCIL ESTATES – CATEGORY I

15 Council estates, well-off older workers
16 Recent council estates
17 Better council estates, younger workers
18 Small council houses, often Scottish

11.2% of England and Wales households

F

COUNCIL ESTATES – CATEGORY II

19 Low rise estates in industrial towns
20 Inter-war council estates, older people
21 Council housing,elderly people

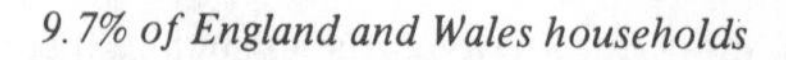

9.7% of England and Wales households

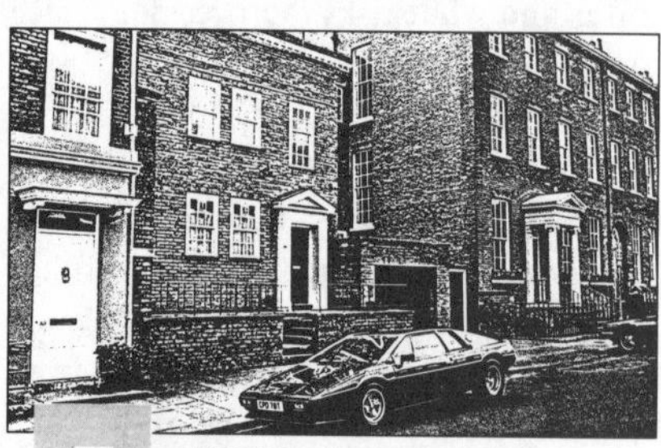

I

HIGH-STATUS NON-FAMILY AREAS

30 High status non-family areas
31 Multi-let big old houses and flats
32 Furnished flats, mostly single people

5.1% of England and Wales households

J

AFFLUENT SUBURBAN HOUSING

33 Inter-war semis, white collar workers
34 Spacious inter-war semis, big gardens
35 Villages with wealthy older commuters
36 Detached houses, exclusive suburbs

16.6% of England and Wales households

C

OLDER HOUSING OF INTERMEDIATE STATUS

8 Mixed owner-occupied and council estates
9 Small town centres and flats above shops
10 Villages with non-farm employment
11 Older private housing, skilled workers

19.7% of England and Wales households

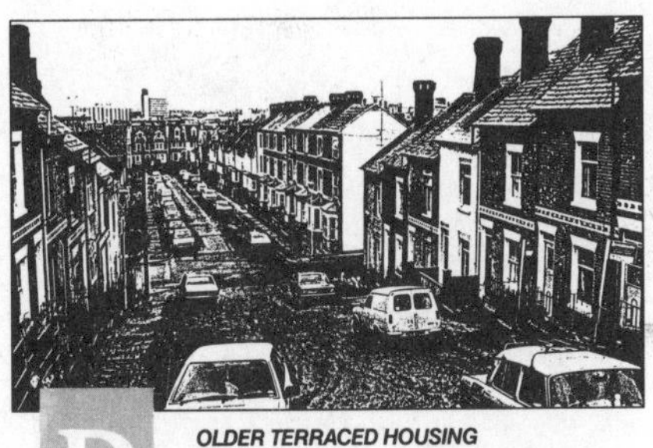

D

OLDER TERRACED HOUSING

12 Unmodernised terraces, older people
13 Older terraces, low income families
14 Tenement flats lacking amenities

4.6% of England and Wales households

G

COUNCIL ESTATES – CATEGORY III

22 New council estates in inner cities
23 Overspill estates, higher unemployment
24 Council estates with some overcrowding
25 Council estates with greatest hardship

5.1% of England and Wales households

MIXED INNER METROPOLITAN AREAS

26 Multi-occupied older housing
27 Cosmopolitan owner-occupied terraces
28 Multi-let housing in cosmopolitan areas
29 Better-off cosmopolitan areas

3.8% of England and Wales households

K

BETTER-OFF RETIREMENT AREAS

37 Private houses, well-off older residents
38 Private flats,older single people

4.6% of England and Wales households

TABLE G.1
Percentage of households in ACORN neighbourhood groups: 1987 England and Wales households, and 1988 BCS core sample

	1987 England and Wales households	*1988 BCS core sample*
	%	%
A. Agricultural areas	3.4	3.5
B. Modern family housing, higher incomes	16.2	14.9
C. Older housing of intermediate status	19.7	19.4
D. Older terraced housing	4.6	5.0
E. Council estates – Category I	11.2	11.5
F. Council estates – Category II	9.7	10.4
G. Council estates – Category III	5.1	5.2
H. Mixed inner metropolitan areas	3.8	3.0
I. High status non-family areas	5.1	4.4
J. Affluent suburban housing	16.6	17.7
K. Better-off retirement areas	4.6	4.7
Unclassified	0.0	0.3

Notes:
1. Estimates of 1987 England and Wales households in different ACORN neighbourhood groups supplied by CACI Market Analysis.
2. Some labels for ACORN neighbourhood groups have been changed by CACI: to remove stigmatising descriptions:
   * Category D – Older Terraced housing – was formerly "Older housing of intermediate status";
   * Category E – Council Estates, Category I – was formerly "Better-off council estates;
   * Category F – Council Estates, Category II – was formerly "Less well-off council estates;
   * Category G – Council Estates, Category III – was formerly "Poorest council estates;
   * Category H – Mixed Inner Metropolitan Areas – was formerly "Multi-racial areas".
3. (not supp) Weighted data, unweighted n = 10,392. Source: 1988 BCS, core sample.

Appendix H
List of publications on the British Crime Survey

The main results of the 1982 and 1984 surveys are reported in, respectively:

Hough, M. and Mayhew, P. (1983). *The British Crime Survey: first report.* Home Office Research Study No. 76. London: HMSO.

Hough, M. and Mayhew, P. (1985). *Taking Account of Crime: findings from the second British Crime Survey.* Home Office Research Study No. 85. London: HMSO.

Some of the other main publications which deal with results from the British Crime Survey, or draw heavily on them, are listed below. They cover results from the 1982 and 1984 surveys.

Publications currently available:

Box, S., Hale, C. and Andrews, G. (1988). 'Explaining fear of crime'. *British Journal of Criminology,* 28,pp. 340-356.

Chambers, G. and Tombs, J. (Eds.) (1984). *The British Crime Survey: Scotland.* A Scottish Office Social Research Study. Edinburgh: HMSO.

Clarke, R.V.G., Ekblom, P., Hough, M. and Mayhew, P. (1985). 'Elderly victims of crime and exposure to risk'. *Howard Journal of Criminal Justice,* 24, pp. 81-89.

Davidson, R. N. (1989). 'Micro-environments of violence'. In, Evans, D.J, and Herbert, D.T., *The Geography of Crime.* London: Routledge.

Elliott, D. and Mayhew, P. (1988). 'Trends in residential burglary: an update. *Home Office Research Bulletin* No. 25. London: Home Office Research and Planning Unit.

Gottfredson, M.R. (1984). *Victims of Crime: the dimensions of risk.* Home Office Research Study No. 81. London: HMSO.

Hope, T. (1988). 'Support for Neighbourhood Watch: a British Crime Survey analysis'. In, Hope, T. and Shaw, M. (Eds.), *Communities and Crime Reduction.* London: HMSO.

Hope, T. (1986). 'Council tenants and crime'. *Home Office Research Bulletin* No. 21. London: Home Office Research and Planning Unit.

Hope, T. (1984). 'Building design and burglary'. In, Clarke, R.V.G. and Hope, T. (Eds.), *Coping with Burglary.* Boston, Mass.: Kluwer-Nijhoff.

Hope, T. and Hough, M. (1988). 'Area, crime and incivilities: findings from the British Crime Survey'. In, Hope, T. and Shaw, M. (Eds.), *Communities and Crime Reduction.* London: HMSO.

Hough, M. and Lewis, H. (1989). 'Counting crime and analysing risks: findings from the British Crime Survey'. In, Evans, D.J. and Herbert, D.T., *The Geography of Crime.* London: Routledge.

Hough, M. (1987). 'Developing a new index of crime: the British Crime Survey'. In, Bradley, U. (Ed.), *Applied Marketing and Social Research.* (2nd Edition). London: Van Nostrand Reinhold.

Hough, M. (1987). 'Offenders' choice of target: findings from victim surveys'. *Journal of Quantitative Criminology,* 3, pp. 355-370.

Hough, M. (1986). 'Victims of violent crime'. In, Fattah, E. (Ed.), *Reorienting the Justice System: from crime police to victim policy.* London: Macmillan.

Hough, M. (1955). 'The impact of victimisation: findings from the British Crime Survey'. *Victimology: an International Journal,* 8, pp. 488-497.

Hough, M. (1984). 'Residential burglary: findings from the British Crime Survey'. In Clarke, R.V.G. and Hope, T. (Eds.), *Coping with Burglary.* Boston, Mass.: Kluwer-Nijhoff.

Hough, M. and Lewis, H (1986) 'Penal hawks and penal doves: attitudes to punishment in the British Crime Survey'. *Home Office Research Bulletin* No. 21. London: Home Office Research and Planning Unit.

Hough, M. and Mo, J. (1986) 'If at first you don't succeed: findings on attempted burglary from the British Crime Survey'. *Home Office Research Bulletin* No. 21. London: Home Office Research and Planning Unit.

Hough, M. and Moxon, D. (1985). 'Dealing with offenders: popular justice and the views of victims'. *Howard Journal of Criminal Justice,* 24, pp. 160-175.

Hough, M., Moxon, D. and Lewis, H. (1987). 'Attributes to punishment'. In, Pennington, R. and Lloyd-Bostock, S. (Eds.), *The Psychology of Sentencing.* Oxford: Centre for Socio-Legal Studies.

Hough, M. and Sheehy, K. (1986) 'Incidents of violence: findings from the British Crime Survey'. *Home Office Research Bulletin* No. 20. London: Home Office Research and Planning Unit.

Lewis, H. and Mo, J. (1986). 'Burglary insurance: findings from the British Crime Survey'. *Home Office Research Bulletin* No. 22. London: Home Office Research and Planning Unit.

Litton, R. (1987). 'Crime and insurance'. *The Geneva Papers on Risk and Insurance.* 12, pp. 198-225.

Maguire, M. and Corbett, C. (1986). *The Effects of Crime and the Work of Victim Support Schemes.* Cambridge Studies in Criminology, 56. Aldershot: Gower. (Chapter 3).

Mawby, R.I. (1988). 'Age, vulnerability and the impact of crime'. In, Maguire, M. and Pointing, J. (Eds.), *Victims of Crime: A New Deal.* Milton Keynes: Open University Education Enterprises.

Maxfield, M.G. (1988). 'The London Metropolitan Police and their clients: victim and suspect attitudes' *Journal of Research in Crime and Delinquency,* 25, pp. 188-206.

Maxfield, M.G. (1987). *Fear of Crime: findings from the 1984 British Crime Survey.* Home Office Research and Planning Unit Paper No. 43. London: Home Office.

Maxfield, M.G. (1987). 'Lifestyle and routine activity theories of crime: empirical studies of victimization, delinquency and offender decision-making'. *Journal of Quantitative Criminology,* 3, pp. 275-282.

Maxfield, M.G. (1987). 'Household composition, routine activity, and victimization: a comparative analysis'. *Journal of Quantitative Criminology,* 3, pp. 301-320.

Maxfield, M.G. (1984). *Fear of Crime in England and Wales.* Home Office Research Study No. 78. London: HMSO.

Mayhew, P. (1987). *Residential Burglary: a comparison of the US, Canada and England and Wales.* National Institute of Justice. Washington, DC: Government Printing Office.

Mayhew, P. (1987). 'How are we faring on the burglary front? A comparison with the US and Canada'. *Home Office Research Bulletin* No. 23. 1987. London: Home Office.

Mayhew, P. (1984). 'Target-hardening: how much of an answer?'. In, Clarke, R.V.G. and Hope, T. (Eds.), *Coping with Burglary.* Boston, Mass.: Kluwer-Nijhoff.

Mayhew, P. and Hough, M. (1988). 'The British Crime Survey: origins and impact'. In, Maguire, M. and Pointing, J. (Eds.), *Victims of Crime: A New Deal.* Milton Keynes: Open University Educational Enterprises.

Mayhew, P. and Smith, L.J.F. (1985). 'Crime in England and Wales and Scotland: a British Crime Survey comparison'. *British Journal of Criminology,* 25, pp. 148-159.

Mott, J. (1985). 'Self-reported cannabis use in Great Britain in 1981'. *British Journal of Addiction,* 80, pp. 37-43.

Moxon, D. and Jones, P. (1984). 'Public reactions to police behaviour: some findings from the British Crime Survey'. *Policing,* 1, pp. 49-56.

Pease, K. (1988). *Judgements of crime seriousness: evidence from the 1984 British Crime Survey.* Home Office Research and Planning Unit Paper No. 44. London: Home Office.

Pease, K. (1986). 'Obscene telephone calls in England and Wales'. *Howard Journal of Criminal Justice,* 24, pp. 275-281.

Riley, D. (1986). 'Drinking drivers: the limits to deterrence?'. *Howard Journal of Criminal Justice,* 24, pp. 241-256.

Riley, D. (1984). 'Drivers' beliefs about alcohol and the law'. *Home Office Research Bulletin,* No. 17. London: Home Office Research and Planning Unit.

Sampson. R.J. (1987). 'Personal violence by strangers: an extension and test of the opportunity model of predatory victimization'. *Journal of Criminal Law and Criminology,* 78, pp. 327-356.

Sampson, R.J. and Wooldredge, J.D. (1987). 'Linking the micro- and macro-level dimensions of lifestyle-routine activity and opportunity models of predatory victimization'. *Journal of Quantitative Criminology,* 3, pp. 371-393.

Smith, S.J. (1987). 'Fear of crime: beyond a geography of deviance'. *Progress in Human Geography,* 11, pp. 1-23.

Smith, S.J. (1987). 'Social relations, neighbourhood structure and the fear of crime in Britain'. In, Evans, D.J. and Herbert, D.T., *The Geography of Crime.* London: Routledge.

Southgate, P. (1984). 'Crime and attitude surveys as an aid to policing'. *Home Office Research Bulletin* No. 18. London: Home Office Research and Planning Unit.

Southgate, P. and Ekblom, P. (1984). *Contacts between Police and Public: findings from the British Crime Survey.* Home Office Research Study No. 77. London: HMSO.

Worrall, A and Pease, K. (1986). 'Personal crimes against women: findings from the 1982 British Crime Survey'. *Howard Journal of Criminal Justice,* 25, pp. 118-124.

Forthcoming publications

Hough, M. (Forthcoming). 'Demand for policing and police performance: progress and pitfalls in public surveys'. In, Weatheritt, M. (Ed.), *Proceedings of a Police Foundation Conference, Harrogate, 1985.* Farnborough: Gower.

Hough. M. (Forthcoming). 'Crime surveys and the measurement of crime'. In, Bluglass, R. and Bowden, T. (Eds.), *Principles and Practice of Forensic Psychiatry.* Edinburgh: Churchill Livingstone.

Mayhew, P. and Elliott, D.P. (Forthcoming). 'Self-reported offending, victimization and the British Crime Survey'. *Victims and Violence.*

Technical reports

Details of the design of the 1988, 1984 and 1982 BCS can be found, respectively, in:

NOP/SCPR (1989). *1988 British Crime Survey Technical Report.*
London:SCPR/NOP Market Research Limited

NOP Market Research Limited. (1985). *1984 British Crime Survey Technical Report.* NOP/9888. London: NOP Market Research Limited.

Wood, D.S. (1983). *British Crime Survey: Technical Report.* London: Social and Community Planning Research.

For a user manual on analysing the 1982 BCS, see:

Hall, J.F. and Walker, A.M. (1985). *User Manual for the first British Crime Survey, 1982.* London: Survey Research Unit, Polytechnic of North London.

References

Austin, C. (1988). *The Prevention of Robbery at Building Society Branches.* Crime Prevention Unit Paper No. 14. London: Home Office.

Bennett, T. (Forthcoming). 'Factors relating to participation in Neighbourhood Watch schemes'. *British Journal of Criminology*, 29.

Bennett, T. (1987). An Evaluation of two Neighbourhood Watch Schemes in London. Cambridge: Institute of Criminology.

Block, C. B. and Block, R. L. (1984). 'Crime definition, crime measurement and victim surveys'. *Journal of Social Issues*, 40, pp. 137-160.

Block, R., Felson, M. and Block, C. R. (1984). 'Crime Victimisation and the United States Occupational Structure: victimisation risk of the civilian labor force'. Paper presented at the annual meeting of the American Society of Criminology, Cincinnati, November 1984.

Bottoms, A. E., Mawby, R. I. and Walker, M. (1987). 'A localised crime survey in contrasting areas of a city'. *British Journal of Criminology*, 27, pp. 125-154.

Box, S., Hale, C. and Andrews, G. (1988). 'Explaining fear of crime'. *British Journal of Criminology*, 28, pp. 340-356.

Brown, C. (1984). *Black and White Britain: the third PSI survey.* London: Heinemann.

Brown, C. and Ritchie, J. (1981). *Focussed enumeration: the development of a method of samping ethnic minorities*. London: Social and Community Planning Research.

Bureau of Justic Statistics (US). (1988). *Report to the Nation on Crime and Justice.* Second Edition. US Department of Justice. Washington DC: Government Printing.

Burrows, J. (1982). 'How crimes come to police notice'. *Research Bulletin,* No. 13. London: Home Office Research and Planning Unit.

Chambers, G. and Tombs, J. (Eds.). *The British Crime Survey: Scotland.* A Scottish Office Social Research Study. Edinburgh: HMSO.

Collins, J. J. and Cox, B. G. (1985). 'Job activities and personal crime victimization: implications of theory'. Social Science Research, 16, pp. 345-360.

Dawson, J. Middleton, S. and Sill, A. (1987). *Fear and Crime in the Inner City.* Community Consultants: the Economic and Social Policy Research Cooperative.

Department of the Environment. (1985). *1981 Based Estimates of Numbers of Households in England, the Regions, Counties and Metropolitan Districts and London Boroughs: 1981-2001*. London: Government Statistical Service.

Dodge, R. and Lentzner, H. (1984). 'Patterns of personal series victimizations in the National crime Survey'. In, Lehnen, R. G. and Skogan, W. G. (Eds.)., *The National Crime Survey: Working Papers*. Vol II: Methodological Studies. Bureau of Justice Statistics, US Department of Justice. Washington, DC: Government Printing Office.

Durant, M., Thomas, M. and Willcock, H. D. (1972). *Crime, Criminals and the Law*. London: HMSO.

Ekblom, C. (1988). *Preventing Robberies at Sub-Post Offices*. Crime Prevention Unit Paper No. 9. London: Home Office.

Ekblom, P. and Heal, K. (1982). *The Police Response to Calls from the Public*. Research and Planning Unit Paper No. 9. London: Home Office Research and Planning Unit.

Elliott, D. and Mayhew, P. (1988). 'Trends in residential burglary: and update. *Home Office Research Bulletin* No. 25. London: Home Office Research and Planning Unit.

Farrington, D. P. and Dowds, E. A. (1985). 'Disentangling criminal behaviour and police reaction'. In Farrington, D. P. and Gunn, J. (Eds.), *Reaction to Crime: the public, the police, courts, and prisons*. Chichester: John Wiley.

Fitzgerald, M. and Ellis, T. (1989). 'Racial harassment: the evidence'. Paper presented to British Criminology Conference, Bristol, July 1989.

Forrester, D., Chatterton, M. and Pease, K. (1988). *The Kirkholt Burglary Prevention Project, Rochdale*. Crime Prevention Unit Paper No. 13. London: Home Office.

Garofalo, J. (1987). 'Reassessing the lifestyle model of criminal victimization'. In, M. Gottfredson and Hirschi, T. (Eds.), Positive Criminology: essays in honor of Michael J. Hindelang. Beverly Hills, CA: Sage.

Gottfredson, M. R. (1986) 'The substantive contribution of victimization survey' In, Tonry, M. H. and Morris, M. (Eds.), *Crime and Justice: an annual review of research*. Vol. 7. Chicago: University of Chicago Press.

Gottfredson, M. R. (1984). *Victims of Crime: the dimensions of risk.*Home Office Research Study No. 81. London: HMSO.

London Borough of Newham. (1987). *Crime in Newham: the survey*. London: London Borough of Newham.

Health Services Advisory Committee (HSAC). (1987). Violence to staff in the health services. Health and Safety Commission. London: HMSO.

Home Office. (1989a). *Notifiable offences recorded by the police*. Quarterly Statistical Bulletin. London: Home Office.

Home Office. (1989b). *Crime Statistics for the Metropolitan Police District by Ethnic Group, 1987: victims, suspects and those arrested*. Statistical Bulletin 5/89. London: Home Office.

Home Office. (1988). *Criminal Statistics, England and Wales, 1987*. Cm. 498. London: HMSO.

Home Office. (1986). *Violent Crime: characteristics of victims and circumstances of recorded offences, 1984*. Statistical Bulletin 29/86. London: Home Office.

Home Office. (1982). *Unrecorded Offences of Burglary and Theft in a Dwelling In England and Wales: estimates from the General Household Survey*. Home Office Statistical Bulletin 11/82. London: Home Office.

Home, T. (1988). 'Support for Neighbourhood Watch: a British Crime Survey analysis'. In Hope, T. and Shaw, M. (Eds.), *Communities and Crime Reduction*. London: HMSO.

Hough, M. and Mayhew, P. (1985). *Taking Account of Crime; findings from the second British Crime Survey*. Home Office Research Study No. 85. London: HMSO.

Hough, M. and Mayhew, P. (1983). *The British Crime Survey: first report*. Home Office Research Study No. 76. London: HMSO.

Husain, S. (1988). *Neighbourhood Watch in England and Wales: a locational analysis*. Crime Prevention Unit Paper No. 12. London: Home Office.

Jones, T., Maclean, B. and Young, J. (1986). *The Islington Crime Survey*. London: Gower.

Johnson, M. and Cross. (1983). 'Surveying service users in multi-racial areas: the methodology of the Urban Institutions project'. Research Papers in Ethnic Relations. Warwick: University of Warwick, Centre for Ethnic Relations.

Kinsey, R. (1985). *Merseyside Crime and Police Surveys: final report*. October 1985. Edinburgh: Centre for Criminology, University of Edinburgh.

Lavrakas, P. J. and Herz, E. (1982). 'Citizen participation in neighbourhood anti-crime measures'. *Criminology*, 20, pp. 479-498.

Laycock, G. (1989). *An Evaluation of Domestic Security Surveys*. Crime Prevention Unit Paper No. 18. London: Home Office.

Laycock, G. (1985). *Reducing burglary: a study of chemists' shops*. Crime Prevention Unit Paper No. 1. London: Home Office.

Lewis, D. A. and Salem, G. (1981). 'Community crime prevention: an analysis of a developing strategy'. *Crime and Delinquency*, 27 pp. 405-421.

Lindsay, B. and McGillis, D. (1986). 'Citywide community crime prevention: an assessment of the Seattle Program'. In, Rosenbaum, D. (Ed.), *Community Crime Prevention: does it work?* Sage Criminal Justice System Annuals, Vol. 22. Beverly Hills: Sage.

Lynch, J. P. (1987). 'Routine activity and victimization at work'. *Journal of Quantitative Criminology*, 3, pp. 283-300.

Maguire, M. and Corbett, C. (1987). *The Effects of Crime and the Work of Victim Support Schemes*. Cambridge Studies in Criminology, 56. Aldershot: Gower.

Mawby, R. I. (1988). 'Age, vulnerability and the impact of crime'. In, Maguire, M. and Pointing, J. (Eds.), *Victims of Crime: A New Deal*. Milton Keynes: Open University Education Enterprises.

Mawby, R. I. (1988). 'Women and crime: from victimization rates to crime experience.' Paper presented to 10th International Congress of Criminology, Hamburg 1988.

Maxfield, M. G. (1987). *Fear of Crime: findings from the 1984 British Crime Survey*. Home Office Research and Planning Unit Paper No. 43. London: Home Office.

Maxfield, M. G. (1984). *Fear of Crime in England and Wales*. Home Office Research Study No. 78. London: HMSO.

Maxfield, M. G. (1984). 'The London Metropolitan Police and two constituencies: victim and suspect attitudes'. *Journal of Research in Crime and Delinquency*, 25, pp. 188-206.

Mayhew, P. (1985). 'The effects of crime: victims, the public and fear'. In, *Research on Victimisation*. Collected Studies in Criminological Research. Vol XXII. Strasbourg: Council of Europe.

Mayhew, P. and Hough, M. (1988). 'The British Crime Survey: origins and impact'. In, Maguire, M. and Pointing, J. (eds.), *Victims of Crime: A New Deal*. Milton Keynes: Open University Education Enterprises.

Mayhew, P. and Smith, L. J. F. (1985). 'Crime in England and Wales and Scotland: a British Crime Survey comparison'. *British Journal of Criminology*, 25, pp. 148-159.

Moxon, D. and Jones, P. (1984). 'Public reactions to police behaviour: some findings from the British Crime Survey'. *Policing*, 1, pp. 49-56.

National Association of Victim Support Schemes (NAVSS). (1988). *Victim Support. Annual Report, 1987/88*. London: NAVSS.

Newburn, T. (1988). *The use and enforcement of compensation orders in magistrates' courts*. Home Office Research Study No. 102. London: HMSO.

Newburn, T. and Merry, S. (Forthcoming). *Keeping in touch: Police victim communication in two areas*. Home Office Research Study. London: HMSO.

NOP Market Research Limited. (1985). *1984 British Crime Survey Technical Report*. NOP/9888. London: NOP Market Research Limited.

NOP/SCPR. (1989). *1988 British Crime Survey Technical Report*. London: SCPR/NOP Market Research Limited.

NRMA Insurance Ltd. (1989). *Car Theft of New South Wales*. Sydney: NRMA Insurance Ltd.

Nuttall, C. P. (1988). 'Crime prevention in Canada'. In Hope, T. and Shaw, M. (Eds.), *Communities and Crime Reduction*. London: HMSO.

Office of Population Censuses and Surveys (OPCS). (1988). 'Mid-1987 population estimates for England and Wales'. London: Government Statistical Service.

Office of Population Censuses and Surveys (OPCS). (1980). *Classification of Occupation, 1980*. London: HMSO.

Painter, K., Lea, J. Woodhouse, T. and Young, J. (1989). *Hammersmith and Fulham Crime and Policy Survey, 1988*. Centre for Criminology. Middlesex: Middlesex Polytechnic.

Parks, R. B. (1976). 'Police response to victimisation: effects on citizen attitudes and perceptions'. In Skogan, W. G. (Ed.), *Sample of Surveys of Victims of Crime*. Cambridge, MA: Ballinger.

Pate, T., Wycoff, M. A., Skogan, W., and Sherman, L. (1986). *Reducing Fear of Crime in Houston and Newark: a summary report*. Washington, DC: Police Foundation.

Pease, K. (1988). *Judgements of crime seriousness: evidence from the 1984 British Crime Survey*. Home Office Research And Planning Unit Paper No. 44. London: Home Office.

Poister, T. H., McDavid, J. C. (1978). 'Victims' evaluation of police performance'. *Journal of Criminal Justice*, 6, pp. 133-149.

Poyner, B., Warne, C., Webb, B., Woodall, R. and Meakin, R. (1988). *Preventing Violence to Staff*. London: HMSO.

Rand, M., Klaus, P., and Taylor, B. (1983). 'The criminal event'. In *Report to the National on Crime and Justice*. Bureau of Justice Statistics. US Department of Justice. Washington, DC: Government Printing Office.

Reiss, A. J. (1986). 'Official and survey crime statistics'. In Fattah, E. (Ed.), *From Crime Policy to Victim Policy*. London: Macmillan.

Rosenbaum, D. P. , Lewis, D. A. and Grant, J. A. (1986). 'Neighborhood-based crime prevention in Chicago: a look at the impact of community organising'. In Rosenbaum, D. P. (Ed), *Community Crime Prevention: does it work?* Beverly Hills, CA.: Sage.

Rosenbuam, D. P. (1988). 'A critical eye on neighbourhood watch: does it reduce crime and fear?' In Hope, T. and Shaw, M. (Eds.), *Communities and Crime Prevention*. London: HMSO.

Shaw, C. (1988). 'Latest estimates of ethnic minority populations'. *Population Trends*, No. 51. London: HMSO.

Skogan, W. G. (1986). 'Methodological issues in the study of victimisation'. In Fattah, E. A. (Ed.), *From Crime Policy to Victim Policy*. Basingstoke: Macmillan.

Skogan, W. G. (1984). 'Reporting crimes to the police: the status of world research'. *Journal of Research in Crime and Delinquency*, 21, pp. 113-137.

Skogan, W. G. (1978). Victimisation Surveys and Criminal Justice Planning. Visiting Fellowship Program Report. US Department of Justice, National Institute of Law Enforcement and Criminal Justice. Washington, DC: Government Printing Office.

Skogan, W. G. and Maxfield, M. G. (1981). *Coping with Crime*. Beverly Hills, CA; Sage.

Smith, D. J. and Gray, J. (1985). *Police and People in London*. Aldershot: Gower.

Smith, L. J. F. (1987). *Crime in Hospitals*. Crime Prevention Unit Paper No. 7. London: Home Office.

Southgate, P. and Ekblom, P. (1984). *Contacts between Police and Public: findings from the British Crime Survey*. Home Office Research Study No. 77. London: HMSO.

Sparks, R. F. (1982). *Research on Victims of Crime: accomplishments, issues, and new directions*. Rockville, MD. National Institute Of Mental Health, Centre for Studies of Crime and Delinquency.

Sparks, R. F., Genn, H. and Dodd, D. J. (1977). *Surveying Victims*. London: John Wiley.

Todd, J. and Butcher, B. (1982). *Electoral Registration in 1981*. Office of Population Censuses And Surveys. London: HMSO.

Tuck, M. and Southgate, P. (1981). *Ethnic minorities, Crime and Policing*. Home Office Research Study No. 70. London: HMSO.

US Department of Justice. (1976). *Criminal Victimization in the United States, 1976*. A National Crime Survey report. Washington DC: Government Printing Office.

Veater, P. (1987). *Evaluation of Kingsdown Neighbourhood Watch Project*. Bristol: Avon and Somerset Constabulary.

Waller, I. (1982). 'Crime victims: needs, services and reforms. Orphans of a social policy'. Paper presented at the IVth International Symposium on Victimology, Tokyo/Kyota, 1982.

Whitaker, C. (1986). *Crime Prevention Measures*. Bureau of Justice Statistics Special Report. Washington, DC: US Department of Justice.

Widom, C. S. And Maxfield, M. G. (1984). 'Sex roles and the victimization of women: evidence from the British Crime Survey'. Paper presented at the Annual Meeting of the American Society Of Criminology, Cincinnati, November, 1984.

Worrall, A. and Pease, K. (1986). 'Personal crimes against women: findings from the 1982 British Crime Survey'. *Howard Journal of Criminal Justice*, 25, pp. 118-124.

Glossary of terms

Acorn – A classification of areas developed by CACI on the basis of selected 1981 Census variables. The eleven ACORN neighbourhood groups have been used in this report. Appendix G gives further details.

Afro-Caribbeans – Used to cover one of the two ethnic minority groups covered in the 'booster' sample. They are people who described themselves as 'black', and therefore will include a number of Africans (about 15% on Labour Force Survey figures).

Asians – Used to cover one of the two ethnic minority groups covered in the 'booster' sample. They are people who described themselves as from India, Pakistan and Bangladesh.

Assault – The term assault covers three sub-categories: serious wounding, involving severe injuries intentionally inflicted; other wounding, which involves less serious injury or severe injuries unintentionally inflicted; and common assaults, which are assaults or attempted assaults resulting in no or negligible injury. The term excludes rape or attempted rape and other sexually motivated attacks.

Attempted burglary – Burglaries where there is clear evidence that the offender made an attempt to gain entry, but did not actually enter the house (see also **Burglary**). The term 'attempted burglary' is also used occasionally in the report to cover attempts and burglaries with entry which did not involve any loss. Another term used for these is 'no-loss burglaries'.

Bicycle theft – Theft of pedal cycles. Thefts which take place inside the house by someone who is not trespassing at the time are counted as 'theft in a dwelling'; and thefts or cycles from inside the house by a trespasser are counted as 'burglary'. The survey covers thefts of bicycles belonging to the respondent or any member of the household.

Booster sample – The additional sample of 1,349 respondents interviewed in the 1988 BCS who were: Afro-Caribbean, Indian, Pakistani, or Bangladeshi. See Appendix C for details of sampling procedures.

Burglary – Entering a dwelling as a trespasser with the intention of committing theft, rape, grevious bodily harm, or unlawful damage, whether the intention is carried through or not. Entry may be by force, through an insecure door or window, or by impersonating a workman, meter reader, etc. The dwelling is a house, flat or any outhouse or garage linked to the dwelling via a connecting door. Temporary residences (hotel rooms, holiday cottages, etc.) also count as targets for burglary. Attempted burglaries (see above) are included with burglaries in this report, unless otherwise specified. Police records cover burglary of other premises (eg. shops, warehouses); in this report only burglary to residential premises are covered, the term burglary being used for all these domestic burglaries.

Common assault – Assault or attempted assault (see **Assault** above) where there was no or negligible injury. Common assaults are summary offences in law and are not treated by the police as 'notifiable offences'.

Core sample – The main 1988 BCS sample of 10,392 respondents which, after appropriate weighting, is a representative cross-section of people aged 16 and over living in private households whose addresses appear in the electoral register. See Appendix C for details of sampling.

Crimes of violence – See **Violent offences** below.

Criminal damage – Usually referred to as vandalism in this report – see **vandalism** below.

Domestic burglary – See **Burglary**.

Ethnic minorities – The additional sample of respondents interviewed in the 1988 BCS who were: Afro-Caribbean, Indian, Pakistani, or Bangladeshi. See also **Booster sample** above.

Household – Defined as all those people who live at the same address, having meals prepared together and with common housekeeping. Members of a household are not necessarily related by blood or marriage. The survey covers only private households, not people living in hostels, institutions, hotels, etc.

Household offences – For the purposes of this report, household offences comprise the following BCS offence categories: bicycle theft, burglary, theft in a dwelling, other household thefts, thefts of and from motor vehicle, and vandalism to household property and motor vehicles. For household offences – where all members of the household can be regarded as victims – the respondent answers on behalf of the whole household.

Household theft – A survey category of household offences covering thefts and attempts from domestic garages, outhouses, sheds, etc. not directly linked to the dwelling, thefts from gas and electricity pre-payment meters, and thefts from outside the dwelling (excluding thefts of milkbottles from the doorstep). The small number of attempted thefts of or from motor vehicles are included among the survey category of other household thefts (see **Motor vehicle thefts** below).

Incidence rates – Incidence rates show the total number of victimisations based on the number in the sample. This takes account of the fact that some people experience more than one offence.

Job-related victimisation – Used to refer to offences against workers which they said were due to the nature of the job they did.

KOS – A 17 category occupational 'order' classification derived from a fuller list of jobs used in the Condensed Key Occupations for Statistical Purposes (KOS) – see OPCS, 1980.

Manual – A social class classification of the head of household, based on the Registrar General's socio-economic grouping (see OPCS, 1980). Manual workers are those with SEG numbers 7-12, 14 and 15. (See also **Non-manual** below.)

Motor vehicles – Unless otherwise specified, these cover cars, vans, motorcycles, scooters, mopeds, etc. either owned or regularly used by anyone in the household. Lorries, heavy vans, tractors, trailers and towed caravans are excluded.

Motor vehicle thefts – These cover two categories: theft or unauthorised taking of a vehicle (where the vehicle is driven away illegally, whether or not it is recovered); and theft from motor vehicles (ie. theft of parts, accessories and contents). If parts or contents are stolen as well as the vehicle being moved, the incident is classified as theft *of* a motor vehicle. No distinction is made between attempted thefts *of* and attempted thefts *from* motor vehicles because it is often very difficult to distinguish these. Attempted offences are usually not included in the separate categories of thefts of and thefts from motor vehicles. In Table 1, for instance, these attempted thefts are included with 'other household thefts'. Table A.3 in Appendix A shows rate of all motor vehicle thefts, including attempts.

Non-manual – A social class classification of the head of household, based on the Registrar General's socio-economic grouping (see OPCS, 1980). Manual workers are those with SEG numbers 1-6, and 13. (See also **Manual** above).

Non-white – A term used to refer to respondents who were in the ethnic groups (ie, Afro-Caribbean, Indian, Pakistani or Bangladeshi) which the booster sample was meant to pick up. See also **White** below.

Notifiable offences – Currently used on *Criminal Statistics* to refer to offences which before 1979 were called 'indictable' and then (briefly) 'serious' offences. They relate to the type of offences recorded by the police the total of which are notified to the Home Office for the compilation of *Criminal Statistics*.

Other personal theft – A survey category referring to theft of personal property away from the home property (eg. handbags from offices), where there was no direct contract between the offender and victim. Only the respondent can be the victim of this crime category.

Personal offences – For the purposes of this report, personal offences comprise the following BCS offence categories: assaults, sexual offences, robbery, theft from the person, and other personal theft. For personal offences, the respondent reported only on his/her experience. Information was also collected on threats. Few of these meet the criteria of any notifiable or non-notifiable offence and are therefore not included in the count of survey offences in Chapter 2. Analysis elsewhere includes threats where specified.

Prevalence rates – Prevalence rates show the percentage of the sample who were a victim once or more of an offence. Unlike incidence rates they take no account of the *number* of victimisations experienced by each person or household.

Recall period – This is the time between 1st January 1987 and the date of the interview at which respondents were asked to report offences they had experienced. As most interviews took place in February and March 1978, the recall period was usually 13-15 months. Only those incidents occurring in 1987 are counted when computing annual rates. Other information about victims and their experiences is usually derived from incidents occurring over the full recall period.

Robbery – Completed or attempted theft of personal property or cash directly from the person, accompanied by force or the threat of force. Robbery should be distinguished from other thefts from the person which involve speed or stealth rather than force or threat.

Sexual offences – Only women were asked about their experience of sexual offences. The sexual offences which were counted as crimes in the survey comprised rape (and attempts), woundings with a sexual motive, and indecent assault, which involve no injury.

Theft from motor vehicles – See Motor vehicle thefts above.

Theft from the person – Thefts or attempted thefts of a purse, wallet, cash etc. by speed or stealth directly from the person of the victim, but without force or the treat of force.

Theft in a dwelling – Theft committed *inside* a home by someone who is entitled to be there at the time of the offence (eg. party guests, workmen, etc.)

Theft of motor vehicles – See **Motor vehicle theft** above.

Threats, threatening behaviour – Verbal threats or intimidating behaviour. The BCS collected information on threats or intimidation to the respondent or threats made to others against the respondent, treating these as personal offences. (If threats or intimidation took place in the course of other offences, they were subsumed by these). Threats have not been included in Chapter 2 as few of them meet the criteria of any notifiable or non-notifiable offence. Threats are included in analysis elsewhere where specified.

Vandalism – Intentional and malicious damage to property – equated with the *Criminal Statistics* category of criminal damage (qv.). Vandalism ranges from arson to graffiti. Cases where there is nuisance only (eg. letting down car tyres) are not included. Where criminal damage occurs in combination with burglary, robbery or violent offences, these take precedence.

Verbal abuse – Abuse by someone with whom the respondent came into contact in his/her job, other than a colleague.

Violent offences – This term is used in the report to refer to: serious and other wounding; robbery and attempts; and sexual offences of all kinds (see **Sexual offences** above).

Weighted data – Raw data from the survey adjusted in various ways at the data processing stage to correct for imbalances introduced in sampling and by the design of the interview. The weights applied are listed in Appendix C.

White – A term used to refer to respondents who say they were white. See also **Non-white** above.

Wounding – See **Assaults** above.

Publications

Titles already published for the Home Office

Studies in the Causes of Delinquency and the Treatment of Offenders (SCDTO)

1. Prediction Methods in relation to borstal training. Herman Mannheim and Lesile T. Wilkins, 1955. viii + 276pp (11 340051 9).
2. * Time spent awaiting trial. Evelyn Gibson. 1960. v + 45pp. (34-368-2).
3. * Delinquent generations. Leslie T. Wilkins. 1960. vi + 20pp. (11 340053 5).
4. * Murder. Evelyn Gibson and S. Klein. 1961. iv + 44pp. (11 340054 3).
5. Persistent criminals. A study of all offenders liable to preventive detention in 1956. W. H. Hammond and Edna Chayen. 1963. ix + 237pp. (34-368-5).
6. * Some statistical and other numerical techniques for classifying individuals. P. McNaughton Smith. 1965. v + 33pp. (34-368-6).
7. Probation research: a preliminary report. Part I. General outline of research. Part II. Study of Middlesex probation area (SOMPA). Steven Folkard, Kate Lyon, Margaret M. Carver and Erica O'Leary. 1966. vi + 58pp. (11 340374 7).
8. * Probation research: national study of probation. Trends and regional comparisons in probation (England and Wales). Hugh Barr and Erica O'Leary. 1966. vii + 51pp. (34-368-8).
9. * Probation Research. A survey of group work in the probation service. Hugh Barr. 1966. vii + 94pp. (34-368-9).
10. * Types of delinquency and home background. A validation study of Hewitt and Jenkins' hypothesis. Elizabeth Field. 1967. vi + 21pp. (34-368-10).
11. * Studies of female offenders. No. 1–Girls of 16–20 years sentenced to borstal or detention centre training in 1963. No. 2–Women offenders in the Metropolitan Police District in March and April 1957. No. 3–A description of women in prison on January 1, 1965. Nancy Goodman and Jean Price. 1967. v + 78pp. (34-368-11).
12. * The use of the Jesness Inventory on a sample of British probationers. Martin Davies. 1967. iv + 20pp. (34-368-12).
13. * The Jesness Inventory: application to approved school boys. Joy Mott. 1969. iv + 27pp. (11 340063 2).

Home Office Research Studies (HORS)

1. * Workloads in children's department. Eleanor Grey. 1969. vi + 75pp. (11 341019).
2. * Probationers in their social environment. A study of male probationers aged 17-20, together with an analysis of those reconvicted within twelve months. Martin Davies. 1969. vii + 204pp. (11 340102 7).
3. * Murder 1957 to 1968. A Home Office Statistical Division report on murder in England and Wales. Evelyn Gibson and S. Klein (with annex by the Scottish Home and Health Department on murder in Scotland). 1969. vi + 94pp. (11340103 5).
4. *Firearms in crime. A Home Office Statistical Division report on indictable offences involving firearms in England and Wales. A.D. Weatherhead and B.M. Robinson. 1970. viii + 39pp. (11 340104 3).
5. * Financial penalties and probation. Martin Davies. 1970. vii + 39pp. (11 340105 1).
6. * Hostels for probationers. A study of the aims, working and variations in effectiveness of male probation hostels with special reference to the influence of the environment on delinquency. Ian Sinclair. 1971. ix + 200pp (11 340106 X).
7. * Prediction methods in criminology – including a prediction study of young men on probation. Frances H. Simon. 1971. xi + 234pp. (11 340107 8).
8. * Study of the juvenile liaison scheme in West Ham 1961-65. Marilyn Taylor. 1971. vi + 46pp. (11 340108 6).

---

* Out of Print.

9. * Exploration in after-care. I – After-care units in London, Liverpool and Manchester. Martin Silberman (Royal London Prisoners' Aid Society) and Brenda Chapman. II–After-care hostels receiving a Home Office grant. Ian Sinclair and David Snow (HORU). III–St. Martin of Tours House, Ayreh Leissner (National Bureau of Co-operation in Child Care). 1971. xi + 140pp. (11 340109 4).
10. A survey of adoption in Great Britain. Eleanor Grey in collaboration with Roland M. Blunden. 1971. ix + 168pp. (11 340110 8).
11. * Thirteen-year-old approved school boys in 1962. Elizabeth Field, W.H. Hammond and J. Tizard, 1971. xi + 46pp. (11 340111 6).
12. Absconding from approved schools. R.V.G. Clarke and D.N. Martin. 1971. vi + 146pp. (11 340112 4).
13. An experiment in personality assessment of young men remanded in custody. H. Sylvia Anthony. 1972. viii + 79pp. (11 340113 2).
14. * Girl offenders aged 17-20 years. I – Statistics relating to girl offenders aged 17-20 years from 1960 to 1970. II – Re-offending by girls released from borstals or detention centre training. III – The problems of girls released from borstal training during the period on after-care. Jean Davies and Nancy Goodman. 1972. v + 77pp. (11 340114 0).
15. * The Controlled trial in institutional research-paradigm or pitfall for penal evaluators? R.V.G. Clarke and D.B. Cornish. 1972. v + 33pp. (11 340115 9).
16. * A survey of fine enforcement. Paul Softley. 1973. v + 65pp. (11 340116 7).
17. * An index of social environment – designed for use in social work research. Martin Davies. 1973. vi + 63pp. (11 340117 5).
18. * Social enquiry reports and the probation service. Martin Davies and Andrea Knopf. 1973. v + 49pp. (11 340118 3).
19. * Depression, psychopathic personality and attempted suicide in a borstal sample. H. Sylvia Anthony. 1973. viii + 44pp. (11 340119 1).
20. * The use of bail and custody by London magistrates' courts before and after the Criminal Justice Act 1967. Frances Simon and Mollie Weatheritt. 1974. vi + 78pp. (11 340120 5).
21. Social work in the environment. A study of one aspect of probation practice. Martin Davies, with Margaret Rayfield, Alaster Calder and Tony Fowles. 1974. ix + 151pp. (11 340121 3).
22. Social work in prison. An experiment in the use of extended contact with offenders. Margaret Shaw. 1974. vii+154pp. (11 340122 1).
23. Delinquency amongst opiate users. Joy Mott and Marilyn Taylor. 1974. vi + 31pp. (11 340663 0).
24. IMPACT. Intensive matched probation and after-care treatment. Vol. I – The Design of the probation experiment and an interim evaluation. M.S. Folkard, A.J. Fowles, B.C. McWilliams, W. McWilliams, D.D. Smith, D.E. Smith and G.R. Walmsley. 1974. v + 54pp. (11 340664 9).
25. The approved school experience. An account of boys' experiences of training under differing regimes of approved schools, with an attempt to evaluate the effectiveness of that training. Anne B. Dunlop. 1974. vii + 124pp. (11 340665 7).
26. * Absconding from open prisons. Charlotte Banks, Patricia Mayhew and R.J. Sapsford. 1975. vii + 89pp. (11 340665 5).
27. Driving while disqualified. Sue Kriefman. 1975. vi + 136pp. (11 340667 3).
28. Some male offenders' problems. I – Homeless offenders in Liverpool. W. McWilliams. II – Casework with short-term prisoners. Julie Holborn. 1975. viii + 80pp. (11 340669 X).
29. * Community service orders. K. Pease, P. Durkin, I. Earnshaw, D. Payne and J. Thorpe. 1975. viii + 80pp. (11 340669 X).
30. Field Wing Bail Hostel: the first nine months. Frances Simon and Sheena Wilson. 1975. viii + 55pp. (11 340670 3).
31. Homicide in England and Wales 1967-1971. Evelyn Gibson. 1975. iv + 59pp. (11 340753 X).
32. Residential treatment and its effects on delinquency. D.B. Cornish and R.V.G. Clarke. 1975. vi + 74pp. (11 340672 X).
33. Further studies of female offenders. Part A: Borstal girls eight years after release. Nancy Goodman, Elizabeth Maloney and Jean Davies. Part B: The sentencing of women at the London Higher Courts. Nancy Goodman, Paul Durkin and Janet Halton. Part C: Girls appearing before a juvenile court. Jean Davies. 1976. vi + 114pp. (11 340673 8).
34. * Crime as opportunity. P. Mayhew, R.V. G. Clarke, A. Sturman and J.M. Hough. 1976. vii + 36pp. (11 340674 6).

---

* Out of Print.

35. The effectiveness of sentencing: a review of the literature. S.R. Brody. 1976. v + 89pp. (11 340675 4).
36. IMPACT. Intensive matched probation and after-care treatment. Vol II – The results of the experiment. M.S. Folkard, D.E. Smith and D.D. Smith. 1976. xi + 400pp. (11 340676 2).
37. Police cautioning in England and Wales. J.A. Ditchfield. 1976. vi + 31pp. (11 340677 2).
38. Parole in England and Wales. C.P. Nuttall, with E.E Barnard, A.J. Fowles, A. Frost, W.H. Hammond, P. Mayhew, K. Pease, R. Tarling and M.J. Weatheritt. 1977. vi + 90pp. (11 340678 9).
39. Community service assessed in 1976. K. Pease, S. Billingham and I. Earnshaw. 1977. vi + 29pp. (11 340679 7).
40. Screen violence and film censorship: a review of research. Stephen Brody. 1977. vii + 179pp. (11 340680 0).
41. Absconding from borstals. Gloria K. Laycock. 1977. v + 82pp. (11 340681 9).
42. Gambling: a review of the literature and its implications for policy and research. D.B. Cornish 1987. xii + 284pp. (11 340682 7).
43. Compensation orders in magistrates' courts. Paul Softley. 1978. v + 41pp. (11 340683 5).
44. Research in criminal justice. John Croft. 1978. iv + 16pp. (11 340684 3).
45. Prison welfare: an account of an experiment at Liverpool. A.J. Fowles. 1978. v + 34pp. (11 340685 1).
46. Fines in magistrates' courts. Paul Softley. 1978. v + 42pp. (11 340686 X).
47. Tackling vandalism. R.V.G. Clarke (editor), F.J. Gladstone, A. Sturman and Sheena Wilson (contributors). 1978. vi + 91pp. (11 340687 8).
48. Social inquiry reports: a survey. Jennifer Thorpe. 1979. vi + 55pp. (11 340688 6).
49. Crime in public view. P. Mayhew, R.V.G. Clarke, J.N. Burrows, J.M. Hough and S.W. C. Winchester. 1979. v + 36pp. (11 340689 4).
50. * Crime and the community. John Croft. 1979. v + 16pp. (11 340690 8).
51. Life-sentence prisoners. David Smith (editor), Christopher Brown, Joan Worth, Roger Sapsford and Charlotte Banks (contributors). 1979. iv + 51pp. (11 340691 6).
52. Hostels for offenders. Jane E. Andrews, with an appendix by Bill Sheppard. 1979. v + 30pp. (11 340692 4).
53. Previous convictions, sentence and reconviction: a statistical study of a sample of 5,000 offenders convicted January 1971. G.J.O. Phillpotts and L.B. Lancucki. 1979. v + 55pp. (11 340693 2).
54. Sexual offences, consent and sentencing. Roy Walmsley and Karen White. 1979. vi + 77pp. (11 340694 0).
55. Crime prevention and the police. John Burrows, Paul Ekblom and Kevin Heal. 1979. v + 37pp. (11 340695 9).
56. Sentencing practice in magistrates' courts. Roger Tarling, with the assistance of Mollie Weatheritt. 1979. vii + 54pp. (11 340696).
57. Crime and comparative research. John Croft. 1979. iv + 16pp. (11 340697 5).
58. Race, crime and arrests. Philip Stevens and Carole F. Willis. 1979. v+69pp. (11 340698 3).
59. Research and criminal policy. John Croft. 1980. iv+14pp. (11 340699 1).
60. Junior attendance centres. Anne B. Dunlop. 1980. v+49pp. (11 340700 9).
61. Police interrogation: an observational study in four police stations. Paul Softley, with the assistance of David Brown, Bob Forde, George Mair and David Moxon, 1980. vii+67pp (ii 340701 1).
62. Co-ordinating crime prevention efforts. F.J. Gladstone. 1980. v+74pp. (11 340702 5).
63. Crime prevention publicity: an assessment. D. Riley and P. Mayhew. 1980. v+47pp. (11 340703 3).
64. Taking offenders out of circulation. Stephen Brady and Roger Tarling. 1980. v+46pp. (11 340704 1).
65. *Alcoholism and social policy: are we on the right lines? Mary Tuck. 1980. v+30pp. (11 340705 X).
66. Persistent petty offenders. Suzan Fairhead. 1981. vi+78pp. (11 340706 8).
67. Crime control and the police. Pauline Morris and Kevin Heal. 1981. v+71pp. (11 340707 6).
68. Ethnic minorities in Britain: a study of trends in their positions since 1961. Simon Field, George Mair, Tom Rees and Philip Stevens. 1981. v+48pp. (11 340708 4).
69. Managing criminological research. John Croft. 1981. iv+17pp. (11 340709 2).

---

*Out of Print.

70. Ethnic minorities, crime and policing: a survey of the experience of West Indians and whites. Mary Tuck and Peter Southgate. 1981. iv+54pp. (11 340765 3).
71. Contested trials in magistrates' courts. Julie Vennard. 1982. v+32pp. (11 340766 1).
72. Public disorder: a review of research and a study in one inner city area. Simon Field and Peter Southgate. 1982. v+77pp. (11 340767 X).
73. Clearing up crime. John Burrows and Roger Tarling. 1982. vii+31pp. (11 340768 8).
74. Residential burglary: the limits of prevention. Stuart Winchester and Hilary Jackson. 1982. v+47pp (11 340769 6).
75. Concerning crime. John Croft. 1982. iv+16pp (11 340770 X).
76. The British Crime Survey: First Report, Mike Hough and Pat Mayhew. 1983. v+62pp. (11 340789 6).
77. Contacts between police and public: findings from the British Crime Survey. Peter Southgate and Paul Ekblom. 1984. v+42pp. (11 340771 8).
78. Fear of crime in England and Wales. Micheal Maxfield. 1984. v+51pp (11 340 772 6).
79. Crime and police effectiveness. Ronald V. Clarke and Mike Hough. 1984. iv+33pp. (11 340773 4).
80. The attitudes of ethnic minorities. Simon Field. 1984. v+50pp. (11 340077 2).
81. Victims of crime: the dimensions of risk. Micheal Gottfredson. 1984. v+54pp. (11 340775 0).
82. The tape recording of police interviews with suspects: an interim report. Carole Willis. 1984. v+45pp. (11 340776 9).
83. Parental supervision and juvenile delinquency. David Riley and Margaret Shaw. 1985. v+90pp. (11 340799 8).
84. Adult prisons and prisoners in England and Wales 1970-82: a review of the findings of social research. Joy Mott. 1985. vi+73pp. (11 340801 3).
85. Taking account of crime: key findings from the 1984 British Crime Survey. Mike Hough and Pat Mayhew. 1985. vi+115pp. (11 340810 2).
86. Implementing crime prevention measures. Tim Hope. 1985. vi+82pp. (11 340812 9).
87. Resettling refugees: the lessons of research. Simon Field. 1985. vi+62pp. (11 340815 3).
88. Investigating burglary: the measurement of police performance. John Burrows. 1986. v+36pp. (11 340824 2).
89. Personal violence. Roy Walmsley. 1986. vi+87pp. (11 340827 7).
90. Police public encounters. Peter Southgate with the assistance of Paul Ekblom. 1986. vi+150pp. (11 340834 X).
91. Grievance procedures in prisons. John Ditchfield and Clair Austin. 1986. vi+78pp. (11 340839 0).
92. The effectiveness of the Forensic Science Service. Malcolm Ramsay. 1987. vi+100pp. (11 340842 0).
93. The police complaints procedure: a survey of complainants' views. David Brown. 1987. v+98pp. (11 340853 6).
94. The validity of the reconviction prediction score Denis Ward. 1987. vi+40pp. (11 340682 X).
95. Economic aspects of the illicit drug market and drug enforcement policies in the United Kingdom. Adam Wagstaff and Alan Maynard. 1988. vii+156pp. (11 340883 8).
96. Schools, disruptive behaviour and delinquency: a review of research. John Graham. 1988. v+70pp. (11 340887 0).
97. The tape-recording of policy interviews with suspects: a second interim report. Carole Willis, John Macleod and Peter Naish. 1988. vii+97pp. (11 340888 9).
98. Triable-either-way cases: Crown Court or magistrates' court? David Riley and Julie Vennard. 1988. v+52pp. (11 340890 0).
99. Directing patrol work: a study of uniformed policing. John Burrows and Helen Lewis. 1988. v+66pp. (11 340891 9).
100. Probation day centres. George Mair. 1988. v+44pp. (11 340894 3).
101. Amusement machines: dependency and delinquency. John Graham. 1988. v+48pp. (11 340895 1).
102. The use and enforcement of compensation orders in magistrates' courts. Tim Newburn. 1988. v+48pp. (11 340896 X).
103. Sentencing practice in the Crown Court. David Moxon. 1988. v+90pp. (11 340902 8).
104. Detention at the police station under the Police and Criminal Evidence Act 1984. David Brown. 1989. v+76pp. (0 11 340908 7).

---

*Out of Print.

105. Changes in rape offences and sentencing. Charles Lloyd and Roy Walmsley. 1989. vi+53pp. (0 11 340910 9).
106. Concerns about rape. Lorna J. F. Smith. 1989. v+48pp. (0 11 340911 7).
107. Domestic violence. Lorna J. F. Smith. 1989. viii+132pp. (0 11 340925 7).
108. Drinking and Disorder: a study of non-metropolitan violence. Mary Tuck. 1989. v+111pp. (0 11 340926 5).

ALSO

Designing out crime. R. V. G. Clarke and P. Mayhew (editors). 1980. vii+186pp. (22 340732 7).
(This book collects, with an introduction, studies that were originally published in HORS 34, 47, 49, 55, 62 and 63 and which are illustrative of the situational approach to crime prevention.)
Policing today. Kevin Heal, Roger Tarling and John Burrows (editors). 1985. v+181pp. (11 340800 5).
(This book brings together twelve seperate studies on police matters produced during the last few years by the Unit. The collection records some relatively little known contributions to the debate on policing.)
Managing criminal justice: a collection of papers. David Moxon (editior). 1985. vi+222pp. (11 340811 0).
(This book collects a number of studies bearing on the management of the criminal justice system. It includes paper by social scientists and operational researchers working within the Research and Planning Unit, and academic researchers who have studied particular aspects of the criminal process.)
Situational crime prevention: from theory into practice. Kevin Heal and Gloria Laycock (editors). 1986. vii+166pp (11 340826 9).
(Following the publication of *Designing Out Crime,* further research has been completed on the theoretical background to crime prevention. In drawing this work together this book sets down some of the theoretical concerns and discusses the emerging practical issues. It includes contributions by Unit staff as well as academics fron this country and abroad.)
Communities and crime reduction. Tim Hope and Margaret Shaw (editors). 1988. vii+311pp. (11 340892 7).
(The central theme of this book is the possibility of preventing crime by building upon the resources of local communities and of active citizens. The specially commisioned chapters, by distinguished international authors, review contemporary research and policy on community crime prevention.)
New directions in police training. Peter Southgate (editor). 1988 xi+256pp. (11 340889 7).
Training is central to the development of the police role, and particular thought and effort now go into making it more responsive to current needs – in order to produce police officers who are both effective and sensitive in their dealing with the public. This book illustrates some of the thinking and research behind these developments.)

The above HMSO publications can be purchased from Government Bookshops or through booksellers.

The following Home Office research publications are available on request from the Home Office Research and Planning Unit, 50 Queen Anne's Gate, London SW1H 9AT.

Research Unit Papers (RUP)

1. Uniformed police work and management technology. J. M. Hough. 1980.
2. Supplementary information on sexual offences and sentencing. Roy Walmsley and Karen White 1980.
3. Board of Visitor adjudications. David Smith, Claire Austin and John Ditchfifeld. 1981.
4. Day centres and probations. Susan Fairhead, with the assistance of J. Wilkinson-Grey. 1981.

---

*Out of Print.

Research and Planning Unit Papers (RPUP)

5. Ethnic minorities and complaints against the police. Philip Stevens and Carole Willis. 1982.
6. *Crime and public housing. Mike Hough and Pat Mayhew (editors). 1982.
7. *Abstracts of race relations research. George Mair and Philip Stevens (editors). 1982.
8. Police probationer training in race relations. Peter Southgate. 1982.
9. *The police response to calls from the public. Paul Ekblom and Kevin Heal. 1982.
10. City centre crime: a situational approach to prevention. Malcolm Ramsay. 1982.
11. Burglary in schools: the prospects for prevention. Tim Hope. 1982.
12. *Fine enforcement. Paul Softley and David Moxon. 1982.
13. Vietnamese refugees. Peter Jones. 1982.
14. Community resources for victims of crime. Karen Williams. 1983.
15. The use, effectiveness and impact of police stop and search powers. Carole Willis. 1983.
16. Acquittal rates. Sid Butler. 1983.
17. Criminal justice comparisons: the case of Scotland and England and Wales. Lorna J. F. Smith. 1983.
18. Time taken to deal with juveniles under criminal proceedings. Catherine Frankenburg and Roger Tarling. 1983.
19. Civilian review of complaints against the police: a survey of the United States literature. David C. Brown. 1983.
20. Police action on motoring offences. David Riley. 1983.
21. *Diverting drunks from the criminal justice system. Sue Kingsley and George Mair. 1983.
22. The staff resource implications of an independent prosecution system. Peter R. Jones. 1983.
23. Reducing the prison population: an explanatory study in Hampshire. David Smith, Bill Sheppard, George Mair and Karen Williams. 1984.
24. Criminal justice system model: magistrates' courts sub-model. Susan Rice. 1984.
25. Measures of police effectiveness and efficiency. Ian Sinclair and Clive Miller. 1984.
26. Punishment practice by prison Boards of Visitors. Susan Iles, Adrienne Connors, Chris May and Joy Mott. 1984.
27. *Reparation, conciliation and mediation. Tony Marshall. 1984.
28. Magistrates' domestic courts: new perspectives. Tony Marshall (editor). 1984.
29. Racism awareness training for the police. Peter Southgate. 1984.
30. Community constables: a study of policing initiative. David Brown and Susan Iles. 1985.
31. Recruiting volunteers. Hilary Jackson. 1985.
32. Juvenile sentencing: is there a tariff? David Moxon, Peter Jones and Roger Tarling. 1985.
33. Bring people together: mediation and reparation projects in Great Britain. Tony Marshall and Martin Walpole. 1985.
34. Remands in the absence of the accused. Chris May. 1985.
35. Modelling the criminal justice system. Patricia M. Morgan. 1986.
36. The criminal justice system model: the flow model. Hugh Pullinger. 1986.
37. Burglary: police actions and victims' views. John Burrows. 1986.
38. Unlocking community resources: four experimental government small grant schemes. Hilary Jackson. 1986.
39. The cost of discriminating: a review of the literature. Shirley Dex. 1986.
40. Waiting for Crown Court trial: the remand population. Rachel Pearce. 1987.
41. Children's evidence: the need for corroboration. Carol Hedderman. 1987.
42. A preliminary study of victim offender mediation and reparation schemes in England and Wales. Gwynn Davis, Jacky Boucherat and David Watson. 1987.
43. Explaining fear of crime: evidence from the 1984 British Crime Survey. Michael Maxfield. 1988.
44. Judgements of crime seriousness: evidence from the 1984 British Crime Survey. Ken Pease. 1988.
45. Waiting time on the day in magistrates' courts: a review of case listing practices. David Moxon and Roger Tarling (editors). 1988.
46. Bail and probation work: the ILPS temporary bail action project. George Mair. 1988.

---

*Out of Print.

47. Police work and manpower allocation. Roger Tarling. 1988.
48. Computers in the courtroom. Carol Hedderman. 1988.
49. Data interchange between magistrates' courts and other agencies. Carol Hedderman. 1988.
50. Bail and probation work II: the use of London probation/bail hostels for bailees. Helen Lewis and George Mair. 1989.
51. The role and function of police community liaison officers. Susan V. Phillips and Raymond Cochrane. 1989.
52. Insuring against burglary losses. Helen Lewis. 1989.

*Out of Print

Research Bulletin

The Research Bulletin is published twice a year and consists mainly of short articles relating to projects which are part of the Home Office Research and Planning Unit's research programme.

Printed in the United Kingdom for Her Majesty's Stationery Office.
Dd 290083 c30 8/89